Debating
Singapore

Debating Singapore
Reflective essays

edited by
Derek da Cunha

 **INSTITUTE OF SOUTHEAST ASIAN STUDIES**

Published by
Institute of Southeast Asian Studies
Heng Mui Keng Terrace
Pasir Panjang
Singapore 0511

The responsibility for facts and opinions expressed in this publication rests exclusively with the authors and their interpretations do not necessarily reflect the views or the policy of the Institute or its supporters.

Cataloguing in Publication Data

Debating Singapore : reflective essays / edited by Derek da Cunha
  1. Singapore — Politics and government — 1965–
  2. Singapore — Social conditions.
  3. Arts — Singapore
  4. Singapore — Economic conditions — 1965–
  I. Da Cunha, Derek.
DS599.64 D28   1994   sls94-41913
ISBN 981-3016-82-5

Typeset by Superskill Graphics Pte Ltd
Printed in Singapore by Chong Moh Offset Printing Pte Ltd

Contents

Introduction

Any foreigner who makes return visits to Singapore every few years would attest to the rapidity with which change takes place in the island republic. Indeed, the Singapore of the early 1990s is already a significantly different place from the Singapore of the 1980s. And the difference lies not merely in changing physical landscape, as relentless development turns the last few pockets of rural land into high-rise residential housing estates, but also in the outlook and attitude of Singaporeans. These latter, perhaps more cerebral, changes are given expression in a variety of ways; in politics, ethnic relations, the arts and culture, and through that all-encompassing term, economics, which is particularly close to the hearts of Singaporeans.

With the remarkable speed that change has been effected in these spheres of Singapore life over the last few years, trying to keep track of events and trends and, more significantly, their points of departure, amounts to a daunting task. To that extent, a number of individuals suggested to me the utility of putting together a compilation of essays, written largely by academics, that would chronicle and analyse some of the more salient changes that have taken place in Singapore from the start of the nineties. This book is a direct response to those suggestions.

The essays in this volume are all drawn from the monthly current affairs publication *Trends*, published by the Institute of Southeast Asian Studies and circulated with Singapore's *Business Times* newspaper. (Between September 1990 and February 1992 *Trends* had circulated with the *Straits Times*.)

I have been associated with *Trends* as its Editor since its very inception in September 1990. As a publication devoted to current affairs, *Trends* usually comprises eight essays of a reflective nature, with one or two focused on Singapore. The 31 essays featured in this volume were chosen from the 52 on Singapore drawn from the first 45 issues of *Trends* (up to January 1994).

Readers will immediately notice that all the essays come in bite sizes. This allows for two things — easy digestibility by the reader, and coverage of a large number of topics by no less than 27 authors.

Apart from light editing to make uniform phrasing and jargon, the essays remain essentially in the form they first appeared in *Trends*. So that the reader is aware of this, and the context in which a particular essay was written, the date and issue number in which an essay was published in *Trends* is appended at the end of each essay.

This book makes no pretensions to filling any lacuna in one's knowledge of the rapidly evolving Singapore story. It is essentially intended to provide a slew of snapshots, analysed and dissected by individuals who, with the exception of six, are Singaporeans.

The visitor to Singapore, the academic, the student, and the general reader may all find something of interest within this compact volume. The division of the book into six categories, from politics to economics, with four to six essays in each category, is intended to reflect the key issues that have shaped the discourse on Singapore by scholars and others over the last four years.

Derek da Cunha

Entreé

chapter 1

The intellectual's role in society

Derek da Cunha

Every intellectual attitude is latently political.
— Thomas Mann

In European society, when one refers to the educated person, one tends to identify him or her immediately as a person of culture and refinement.

In modern East Asian society, however, the educated person is almost always identified with the stack of degree certificates he or she has acquired from a clutch of universities.

The situation, though, is now beginning to change: the vast increase in the number of people with university degrees (almost every other business executive has an MBA) is forcing a reassessment of the criteria used to judge a person's worth.

Employers looking for middle-ranking executives want more than just desiccated walking calculators. They want people who exude a certain deportment, flair and verbal skill that are the hallmarks of an intellectual; for it is these attributes which, taken together, are becoming one of the new currencies of power.

Intellectuals, however, are not easy to come by. The more professional types — those who make a profession of intellectualism

— are drawn from the scholarly and cultural communities. And that immediately begs the question: what precisely is the role, if any, of the intellectual in society?

To the extent that the intellectual's role can be defined, it might read something like this:

- to cultivate a habit of independent thinking within a people;
- to challenge those individuals who are more used to having their ideas unchallenged;
- to cast a critical eye over the work of others; and
- to provide a second and far more expansive sounding board for those who generally have a narrow conception of society's needs.

Using such criteria, intellectuals in Singapore have been more of a failure than a success, and they have been roundly and justifiably attacked; indeed, some prominent Singaporeans recently described intellectuals in such terms as "idle academics", and as a group which "has not contributed enough to the intellectual climate here".

This is fair comment, although the fault may not lie entirely with the intellectuals themselves. For the fact of the matter is that in a small, Asian society, people's sensitivities are far more acute and reactive and often have the unfortunate effect of adversely impinging on the relationship with others.

To that extent, there are enough prickly politicians, bureaucrats and artists around who are quick to take umbrage when their work and policies are challenged and criticized by intellectuals. These people are mostly of a deeply suspicious, insecure and unimaginative cast of mind. Instead of being offended, they ought to switch to more sedate pursuits — like needlework — rather than stick to professions where criticism should be seen as a necessary occupational hazard, and where there is really no place for fragile personalities.

This observation is especially apposite at a time when society is getting more frivolous, people's attention spans are getting shorter, "practised spontaneity" (where individuals are always waiting for a cue from upon high before acting) is being entrenched, and where the "culture of looks" — mere surface impressions — is placed at a premium.

If society is all about tinsel and glitter and mere material well-being to the total exclusion of intellectual development and spiritual fulfilment, then the question arises: will people ever be fully satisfied? Unlikely.

And here the job of the intellectual is to occasionally provide a gentle reminder to society that there is something to be said for self-esteem — where an individual may not be adorned with great material wealth, but what adornments he does possess he wears on his heart and expresses through his intellect.

In the final analysis, it is arguable that the inspirational oratory of an intellectual might be more effective in setting ablaze the imagination of a people and evoking in them an aesthetic experience — something intrinsic and far more lasting than the transitoriness that attends the reduction of every issue and argument to either a sense of fear or to purely economic terms.

Society, or at least sections of it, awaits the arrival of more such individuals, and in their wake might well come a not undesirable consequence — a moralistic revival.

Trends, No. 36, *Business Times*, weekend edition, 28–29 August 1993

Democracy under scrutiny

chapter 2

Give me liberty or give me wealth

Russell Heng

An oddity of Singapore politics prompts this essay. Here is a country whose economic achievements fast approach and, in some instances, match the standards of the industrialized democracies but whose politics retain authoritarian vestiges frequently associated with the Third World. Power is overwhelmingly in the hands of one political party, opposition parties are inconsequential, and civil society, broadly described as independent institutions such as trade unions, free churches, liberal professions, and autonomous universities, is weak.

These statements must come with some qualifications. The very powerful People's Action Party (PAP) is freely elected, opposition parties are legal, and public opinion is becoming more lively.

But all things considered, one question can still be asked of an affluent Singapore: why hasn't its political culture caught up with its possessions?

This is hewing closely to liberal development theory, which believes that rising living standards will bring about a demand for more political rights. To be fair, events in Singapore through the 1980s do prove this theory somewhat.

Through two general elections, a generation of young voters brought up in affluence swung 13 per cent of the popular vote away from the PAP. They forced the party to rethink its hitherto autocratic style of government. In the words of Prime Minister Goh Chok Tong in 1987, when he was First Deputy Prime Minister, his government was facing "a new phenomenon of a new society, a middle class society". He recognized that members of such a society did not want the state to shove decisions on them.

The middle class society has required Mr Goh's government to solicit public opinion actively. Censorship, too, has had to be relaxed. But major injunctions remain. For example, professional bodies still cannot freely comment on political issues outside their professional interests except through officially-endorsed channels such as select committee hearings. And new injunctions have been added, such as the act separating religion from politics, which may make religious organizations wary about espousing some of their liberal causes lest such activities be construed as involvement in politics.

More people are speaking up but there is a discernible impression that the voices are coming mainly through co-opted channels such as the government's Feedback Unit.

Of course, this does not necessarily make the opinions any less useful, but co-option is not quite participation in the strictest sense of the word. Take the example of the new species in Parliament known as the Nominated MP: he or she can contribute to debate but he or she is not quite the same as a fully-elected MP.

The pace of change in the Singapore polity becomes even more measured when viewed alongside events in South Korea and Taiwan. The comparisons have been made often enough for reasons which are easy to understand.

All three are Newly Industrializing Economies (NIEs). They are Sinicized societies which have or had authoritarian governments. This and the practice of free market economics are said to have propelled them on to fast economic growth. Both in Taiwan and South Korea rising affluence has created a middle class which has been instrumental in forcing the pace of democratization.

But why have the middle class societies of Seoul and Taipei been that much more clamourous than their counterpart in Singapore? The reasons are not always straightforward.

For instance, the quiescence of Singapore's Chinese-dominated society can no longer be explained by its "Confucianist cultural background". Whether or not Chinese Singaporeans are sufficiently Confucianist is debatable in the first instance.

If there is indeed a legacy of respect for authority passed down from the sage, how does one explain the defiant behaviour in Taiwan and South Korea, which are probably more Confucianist than a Singapore where an English education system has diluted the Chineseness of its ethnic Chinese majority.

So what are the real differences that set Singapore apart from the other two NIEs? Size is one obvious factor. With larger populations, the middle classes of Taiwan and South Korea have the critical mass to be a political force. A larger geographical area also means that power is diffused between the centre and the regions, rather than concentrated, as it would be in a smaller place.

This dimension is present in both Taiwan and South Korea and gives their opposition forces more room for manoeuvre. In fact, during the 1989 elections in Taiwan, the main opposition party used the strategy of capturing regional seats of authority to surround the central government in Taipei.

Yet another significant difference is legitimacy. According to theory, participation comes more readily to people when the regime they face has a problem with legitimacy. The Kuomintang (KMT) in Taiwan, with its pretensions of representing the whole of China, runs a National Assembly where a vast majority of its members had not been elected in 40 years.

South Korea had long years of military government. The government has overcome the problem of legitimacy with free elections, but years of student activism before that have spawned a strong agitprop culture of the streets.

On the other hand, the PAP government has always been elected by a free and fair vote, whatever its critics may say about its authoritarian ways.

If illegitimate government provokes a stronger reaction from the public, so would regimes which are more draconian. That is to say, they used to treat political opposition a lot tougher in Taiwan and South Korea than the PAP ever did in Singapore. Taiwan has its February 28 incident and South Korea the riots at Kwangju, to name just two instances of violent crackdowns on dissidence.

Bloodshed creates martyrs who are powerful symbols for galvanizing anti-establishment emotions. To put it tersely, if the PAP has not aroused such a high level of public dissent, it is because it is not quite repressive enough. Nobody disappears in the night to become a non-person, political dissidents are not executed, and nobody has died in detention.

This is not to say that the Internal Security Act is not intimidating. It is, and its use in recent years has generated unhappiness. But by and large people find it possible to live with the Act, and if fear remains a factor hindering political participation, a question seldom asked is: is it because there is much to fear or is it because it does not take much to frighten Singaporeans?

Indeed, courage does not seem to occupy a very prominent place in Singapore's history. When faced with a set of real nasty rulers as in the Japanese Occupation, the popular memory is rendered in terms of how much people suffered rather than how hard they fought.

Today's political leaders like to point to the anti-British independence movement and how challenging those times were. Indeed they were turbulent times, but the PAP founding members who emerged from that struggle are widely admired for being shrewd, capable, conscientious, determined, and even lucky. They are not quite national heroes, at least not of the blood, sweat and tears category. History has not been generous with inspiring symbols of courage.

Citizens are more prone to be restive when grievances are large. In Singapore, the PAP is very proficient at pre-empting discontent.

One of its greatest achievements is to make house ownership possible for 80 per cent of the population. Housing in both Seoul and Taipei is, however, fast moving beyond the reach of the middle class.

Singapore's government also plants trees and cleans rivers without the blandishments of an environment lobby. Again, the experience of South Korea and Taiwan is very different: there, environmental groups were radicalized by the destruction of the environment for economic development.

The list can go on about the dissimilarities between Singapore's political background and that of the other two places. Sorting out these disparities would be incomplete if nothing is said about the different results that are being witnessed in the three places.

If the Taiwanese and South Koreans are enjoying exhilarating new standards of democracy, they are also grappling with the industrial and social unrest that have come with the removal of old strictures.

Indeed, a lesson emerging from the troubled headlines of Seoul and Taipei would be that too much liberty can be seen to be mucking things up. And if the perspective is cast broader to include the countries of Eastern Europe, political liberties seem to have an inverse relationship with economic efficiency although the initial premise was that democratization was essential for free market economics to succeed.

In effect, the implication seems to be one where choices are stark: give me liberty or give me wealth. The two assets must be traded off, one for the other. Scholars in China have coined the term "neo-authoritarianism" to describe such a system, where politics is tightly regulated so that there is stability for free market economics to be implemented and thus generate wealth.

It is tempting to see this as a form of smaller and milder ideological struggle after the much-talked-about trouncing of communism by democratic capitalism at the end of the last decade. Is democracy's new challenger "neo-authoritarianism"?

This essay will not hazard a guess on how the future will pan out. What is likely is that observers will continue to compare developments in Singapore and the other two NIEs, and look at the failings of one as highlighting the strengths of the other. There is nothing wrong with that as, in a tightly-meshed world, political lessons can cross borders.

Finally, whatever the conclusions may be, Singaporeans should ponder the dark side of this stable and orderly polity which they currently enjoy. A government that makes so many decisions, even if they are right ones, breeds highly dependent and low-participating citizens.

This leads us to one important question: is this political climate conducive to producing enough political talent to run the country? If the PAP with its vast resources admits to problems in recruitment, there is no cause for self-congratulation.

Trends, No. 8, *Sunday Times*, 28 April 1991

chapter 3

Nominated MPs: some check is better than no check

Walter Woon

Why do we need an opposition in Singapore, when we have such an efficient, honest and incorruptible government? This is the usual question posed to the electorate come election time. The answer depends on what the opposition is for. The traditional role of a parliamentary opposition is to oppose. Whether they oppose the government on good grounds is often a secondary consideration; the primary consideration is, will it get them votes? A parliamentary opposition with a real chance of getting into power is possibly the worst thing for a country in the early stages of its economic development. In such cases, the government of the day (it may not be there tomorrow) will flinch from necessary but unpopular policies in order not to alienate the voters. The result is fatal vacillation; fatal because sooner rather than later the economy will grind to a halt, unless the country has enormous natural resources to fall back on.

Unadulterated party politics is a game for the rich. It is perhaps instructive that of the four so-called Little Dragons, not one is a democracy in the full free-wheeling liberal Western sense. This, I think, suits Singapore just as well. It is cold comfort to be held up as a shining example of liberal democracy while having at the same time to beg for your daily bread from the rich.

But this does not mean that we do not need an opposition. Democracy is not the natural state of man. Put a person in a position of unchecked power and one of two things will happen eventually: (1) he becomes dishonest and starts to work the system for his benefit or the benefit of his cronies; or (2) while not being actively dishonest, he becomes intellectually flabby and ceases to think things through with the same thoroughness since there is no one to call him to account.

So far in Singapore we have been largely spared the first scenario (at least, no evidence has surfaced to suggest otherwise). It is the second scenario that we should be concerned about. For the last 30 years Singaporeans have been fortunate against all odds in having an administration that has generally done the right thing. It would be tempting fate to complacently assume that this will continue for the next 30 years.

The nub of the problem is that the new generation of leaders has never had to face any real opposition to their policies. They do not have to justify what they do except to their own backbenchers in Parliament, which is preaching to the converted. You cannot rely on the government's own backbenchers to keep the government in check. The party whip will keep them in line, and under Singapore's Constitution expulsion from one's party means that one's seat in Parliament becomes vacant.

To the credit of the ruling party, they have done some things to ensure an opposition. First, there was the concept of the Non-constituency MP. Now there is the Nominated MP scheme. Purists may decry these measures as being merely cosmetic and not truly democratic in the Westminster or Washington sense. My attitude is purely pragmatic: some check is better than no check and a tame opposition is better than no opposition.

In any case, this is pre-judging the matter. Potentially, the Nominated MPs may wield considerable influence. They are beholden to no political party for their posts and can speak their minds. Unlike the Non-constituency MPs who, by definition, are members of the political opposition, the Nominated MPs do not necessarily have the overthrow of the government in mind when they voice dissent about policies. Given strong personalities, Nominated MPs may exercise influence on public opinion far outstripping that of even ministers.

For the foreseeable future, I think that the only real political opposition to the government will come from the Nominated MPs. The Elected President may also come to take on this role, but it is too early to tell. There has been a great amount of scepticism about the Nominated MP scheme. Many see it as a ploy on the part of the government to diffuse the pressure for a true opposition by setting up a team of straw men. People who could make excellent Nominated MPs may be deterred from accepting nomination because of this scepticism. This is highly regrettable.

Many think that the only "respectable" opposition MP is one who has beaten the government candidate fair and square. Given the usual rag-tag ensemble that runs in elections, I do not think that we are going to get many "respectable" opposition members in the near future. In any case, voting for opposition candidates for the sole reason that they are opposition candidates is hardly a rational way to use one's precious vote.

As things stand now, I do not think that any reasonable person wants the PAP out of office. The alternatives are too gruesome to even contemplate. A time may eventually come when an opposition party can field a team able to provide an alternative government. But this will not happen tomorrow. It may not ever happen at all if the PAP continues to deliver the goods in the economic sense.

For most people, the bottom line is economic well-being. Having an opposition is nice, but not if it means a cut in living standards. The idealists who call for an effective elected parliamentary opposition are baying for the moon. For now, we will have to make do with what we have: Nominated MPs and an effective, independent Elected President. These two institutions can become significant if

chapter 4

Foolish to hamper democracy's growth

Russell Heng

There is a view abroad that the West, in general, and America, in particular, have no business imposing their democratic and human rights standards on other countries. It is also a concern which regularly gets an airing in Singapore. Rigorous, well-publicized arguments to this end have been raised by officialdom and the media here. Readers who follow this issue should be familiar with the details and I shall assume a summary is unnecessary.

What this essay seeks to do is to take what is essentially a strategic issue away from a protracted debate on rights and wrongs (i.e. is the West hypocritical in demanding human rights and so forth?) back to where it should belong: the strategic gains and losses of promoting democracy world-wide.

This rather more down-to-earth approach may find a keener understanding within the Singapore mind-set. A useful analogy to draw would be the ease with which officialdom in Singapore grasps the necessity of a global U.S. military presence, particularly in this part of the world, and how it contributes to regional stability as well as the country's security.

It is even more significant that this perspective has been maintained at some cost to the Republic's relationship with some of its neighbours but, nevertheless, held it Singapore did, and with a conviction that it had got its strategic calculations right.

The point Singapore argues is that removing any U.S. military presence would create a power vacuum. This removal would be inherently destabilizing because others would aspire to fill this vacuum or just fish in troubled waters. However, it is a logic which either fails or refuses to recognize the parallel that if democracy were to withdraw to its Western heartland and leave the world well alone, a similarly unstable vacuum will be created.

Call this a political, ideological or even ethical vacuum, and think of a world where the Western democracies are not there to solve refugee problems or provide relief for disasters. More specifically and closer to home, think of the Cambodian conflict which ultimately relied on a basic mechanism of Western democracy — popular elections to reach a settlement.

Detractors may point out that the promised elections appear unlikely to bring about a real settlement. But if there was a solution to be fashioned from Cambodian folk-ways or Asian political traditions, none of the Asian parties to the conflict, Singapore included, cared to identify it. Flawed as democracy may be, it is sometimes the only acceptable option available. Remove it and there is nothing else. If that is not a vacuum, what do you call it?

Let's return to the analogy of the U.S. military presence. Some countries against such a presence have argued that local forces and not those of any external superpower are the rightful custodians of regional security. This is a position which Singapore policy-makers are uncomfortable with. It would pay them to stretch that wariness to consider a Southeast Asia where no quarter is given to Western democratic and humanitarian influence. Would that make for a more comfortable geopolitical environment for the Republic?

Some thought should well be given to those waiting to fill that vacuum if Western democratic values beat a retreat. Think about that rather extreme form of Islam which is frightening both Islamic and non-Islamic countries. Also, would a stronger China and a resurgent Japan be purveyors of benign political values or, if you must, would they be less disruptive than the United States is sometimes made out to be in some quarters in Singapore?

Why is there this Singapore paradox: seeing the strategic value of an American military presence but not too willing to acknowledge the contributions of its political ethos to international stability? One possible reason is not often stated. An American military presence does not interfere with how power is dispensed in Singapore but American democratic values does sometimes challenge that.

To be fair, there are genuine and valid concerns of how a proselytizing America may be unhelpful to the stability of some countries not yet ready for a free-wheeling liberal polity. There is also a case to be made for urging common sense on the Clinton Administration in its implementation of a human rights policy.

But if we in Singapore decry Western humanitarian concerns too loudly and too frequently, we may one day look back and realize that such haranguing of the Western democracies and discounting of the importance of human rights is a strategic miscalculation. Never mind the ethical question.

Trends, No. 31, *Business Times*, weekend edition, 27–28 March 1993

chapter 5

A minimum working hypothesis of democracy for Singapore

Janadas Devan and Geraldine Heng

Numerous articles have appeared recently in the local media on the subject of democracy. Unfortunately, more heat than light has been generated. As so often happens when human passions engage abstractions, many were tempted to draw the wrong conclusions from correct premises, or offer questionable reasons for sound opinions.

The unavoidable facts about our society were thus lost in the discussion. It took Mr Russell Heng, for instance, in his article "Foolish to hamper democracy's growth", to point out that whatever one might think of Western democracies, Singapore's security depends to a large extent on those same democracies. It is useless to engage in a debate on democracy if we forget such fundamentals in pursuing our disagreements.

Indeed, the debate is only of use if we remind ourselves, once in a while, of what we do agree upon. It is dangerous to debate the claims of democracy, something schoolchildren pledge themselves to everyday, without attempting a minimum working hypothesis to which all parties might accede. What, then, is the most basic thing about democracy as a universal value? And what are the most fundamental facts about Singapore's history which will determine the future of democracy here?

But firstly, the issue that has bedevilled the debate thus far: what, precisely, is the link between democracy and socio-economic progress? We must begin by facing the uncomfortable truth squarely: there is no inevitable link.

The recent history of East Asia, in particular, shows that the fundamentals of development — political stability, social discipline, education — while not incompatible with a fully functioning democracy, can in fact be achieved without the paraphernalia of democracy in place. Indeed, as the countries of Eastern Europe are now discovering, the unsettling effects of democracy can obstruct rather than accomplish these fundamental goals.

In many of these countries, the collapse of communist dictatorships has made the material conditions of life worse, not better. The resplendent hope of no more than three years ago has turned out, in the cold light of day, to have been at best an ethereal rumour.

We should not conclude, however, that the failure of particular democracies renders the democratic ideal itself useless. For one thing, there is at present no convincing alternative ideal on the international scene. Even those who object to the Western view of democracy justify their position by referring, not to the evils of democracy, but to the limitations social realities pose to the immediate fulfilment of democratic ideals in their societies.

The advocates of a so-called Asian democracy, for instance, do not reject democratic ideals as such, but offer rather a re-reading of the democratic ethos that they believe fits better the specificities of Asian cultures. Democracy cannot be utterly bankrupt when all sides of the debate think it incumbent on themselves to invoke democracy.

More seriously, beyond the thrusts and feints of recent debate, a potentially broad democratic consensus exists when we turn our sights from shining abstractions to the pragmatics of socio-economic development.

We can all concede readily enough that one-person-one-vote does not lead inevitably to high per capita income. We can also all agree that dictatorships have not had remarkable socio-economic success either. These are both empirically verifiable facts.

Singaporean critics of democracy have therefore proposed what they call "good government" as the appropriate model of socio-economic development. Advocates of democracy can meet them on this honestly. For when we seek a definition of what constitutes the goals of "good government", what we discover are democratic ideals defined in pragmatic, instrumental terms. Nobody — right or left, conservative or liberal — can disagree with these aims: social justice, economic enfranchisement, equal opportunity.

These are, pre-eminently, democratic expectations whose historical antecedence is fairly recent. It was only in the eighteenth century, with the American and French Revolutions, that these expectations began to be accepted as the *raison d'être* of governments. The nationalist movements that swept through Asia and Africa this century merely confirmed the force of these expectations. Though most post-colonial governments have honoured them more in the breach than in the observance, their universal impetus cannot be denied.

No authority, East or West, can survive for long now if it does not go some way towards meeting them. The astonishing spread of these expectations — at a speed which no religion in history can equal — represents one of the most powerful forces in the world today.

The tremendous developments in contemporary China, for example, may have very little to do with democracy as it is understood on Capitol Hill. But it has everything to do with democracy as a historical force: namely, the belief that every single Chinese, all 1.2 billion of them, has as much right to happiness as the emperors of old or 250 million Americans today. It was only the rare Chinese a century ago who assumed that that right was his. Against this historically unprecedented assumption, the issue of whether every Chinese citizen also has the vote is for the present a mere footnote in history. The essence of democracy — the belief that every individual has an equal claim on the future — has already taken root in China, as it has in India and the rest of Asia. That belief, more than anything else, will determine the course of the next century, which will be more, not less democratic than the present.

And what is true on the world stage is truer still for Singapore. Even as we debate the claims of particular forms of democracy, we should beware that we do not lose sight of the main impetus of our own history. That history, warts and all, is for the most part democratic — or there would have been no Singapore at all. The achievements we are proudest of — public housing, universal education, equal opportunity — are all democratic achievements. Barring a cataclysm, the transformation these achievements have wrought is irreversible.

We cannot cease being democratic when the democratic ethos has already transformed life in the most radically material of ways. The future of democracy in Singapore, whatever the qualms some might have about the value of democracy, has already been determined by the past. If that past is any guide, the future must be more democratic, not less, if Singapore is to exist.

As it is, we tend to underestimate the democratic transformation of Singapore. For different reasons, critics as well as defenders of the Singapore Government are both equally reluctant to admit the full scope of that transformation.

We are all fond of asserting, for instance, that strong and stable government was what changed Singapore. Though that is undoubtedly true, it is equally true that we have stable government not in spite of democracy but because of democracy. In Singapore's case, which is by no means replicable elsewhere, it could not have been otherwise.

Long years with one party in power has in fact led us to forget that stable government was not achieved overnight. A reign of peace and plenty was not installed suddenly on 5 June 1959, when the People's Action Party (PAP) took office. Years of the most extraordinarily intense political struggle followed when the outcome might well have been different. By Mr Lee Kuan Yew's own estimation, it was not till July 1965 — when the PAP won the by-election at Hong Lim, a constituency it had lost twice before — that the PAP secured the trust of the population. Nothing could have been achieved if that trust had not been gained democratically.

Admittedly, stability of government was not established solely through democratic means. But that stability would have been hollow if it had not been based on a democratically-secured mandate. An innately sceptical, independent, rambunctious immigrant citizenry could not have been led without its consent. Things would have fallen apart if the population had not been democratically mobilized.

We should not forget these overwhelming facts about Singapore's political history even as we debate the claims of democracy. That debate is irrelevant unless it acknowledges the facts of our own history: the democratization of socio-economic life in the most material of ways, and the process by which that democratization was achieved, could only have resulted in the deepening of the democratic ethos.

Inevitably, therefore, the political agenda in the near future will be shaped to a significant extent by one question: how will the political system respond to the increasingly insistent democratic demands of a population already accustomed to democratic expectations?

Trends, No. 33, *Business Times*, weekend edition, 29–30 May 1993

chapter 6

For a communitarian democracy in Singapore

Chua Beng Huat

Since the review of the education system in the late 1970s undertaken by Dr Goh Keng Swee, which noted the need for moral education, the People's Action Party (PAP) has been searching for an ideology for Singapore that transcends the pragmatism that had served the nation well in the first two decades of economic development. This search culminated in the adoption of the White Paper on Shared Values in January 1991.

The underlying concept of Shared Values is "communitarianism". The government sees it as the encompassing value that is embraced by all three major racial/cultural groups in the population. It further claims that communitarianism is the cultural essence of Asian societies. Given the vast cultural diversities across Asia, this claim, which eliminates the differences, unavoidably raises debates on its accuracy.

However, what is important is its commitment to a communitarian ideology that is indutiably anti-liberal. Indeed, its dis(re)covery began with the rejection of what the government saw as the creeping insinuation of liberal individualism into the ethos of Singaporeans who, because of their integration into the global economy, were vulnerable to this cultural invasion from Western nations.

We need to take the government's determination to inscribe communitarianism in society seriously and examine its implications for the development of the Singapore polity.

Central to communitarianism is the idea that collective interests be placed above individual ones. Logically, the substance of collective interests should be based on the consensus of the collective itself. However, within a modern state, rationalized on the technical difficulty of soliciting opinions from all interested and affected parties, the elected political leadership readily assumes for itself the position of defining the national interests for the governed. There is thus a conflation of government and society.

This conflation of government/society enables the elected to slip into authoritarianism, either in a genuine belief of acting in the collective welfare or merely using it in a self-serving fashion. The result is an interventionist state which justifies the interventions as pre-emptory good measures to ensure collective welfare. Thus, while logically communitarianism does not favour any form of government, in practice it often spawns authoritarianism.

At the current conjuncture, in spite of an overwhelming elected parliamentary majority, the PAP government has responded more openly to the voices from the ground and has moved towards greater consultation in the formation of consensus on national interests. The question that faces Singapore's political development under a single party-dominant government with a communitarian ideology is, therefore, one of developing political institutions that can hold off the possible imposition of authoritarianism. There are three obvious candidate institutions.

Institutions for a communitarian democracy

First is, of course, election as the means of selecting political leadership within a multi-party political system; without it, democracy is fatuous. Ironically, it took the declines in the PAP's electoral support over the last decade to convince sceptics that election in Singapore is more than a veil for authoritarianism.

Observers marvelled at the seriousness with which the PAP took to heart every percentage point lost, since the losses did not translate into proportional opposition representation in Parliament. This reaction to every small shift of electoral sentiment is partly the result of the PAP's communitarian ideology.

As non-PAP votes constitute protests against the Party, its increased volume stands as an indication of the "absence" of consensus, thus weakening the PAP government's claim to be the embodiment of the "collective interests". Electoral support is thus not about how well the opposition parties do but how united is the nation behind the PAP leadership and the Party's self-characterization as a "people's movement".

Second may be called the "right to be consulted". Within communitarianism there is little conceptual space for individual rights. Constrained within the conceptual space of collective interests, no individual or group can assert its own right as a basic condition of existence, lest the assertion be read as unacceptable self-interest, potentially detrimental to the whole. However, as consensus is required, legitimate interest groups have the right to be consulted in consensus formation.

This right differs from liberal concepts of individual rights, which are conceived as "transcendental" and "natural" rights to be protected against state infringement. In contrast, it is constituted pragmatically, on grounds that consensus can emerge only when all identifiable interested parties are consulted and differences accommodated where possible. Similarly, and not on liberal premises, the rights to interest group formation and representation have to be institutionalized.

As the inscription of communitarianism is a recent phenomenon in Singapore, the right to be consulted is not yet firmly institutionalized. This is reflected in the government's continuing refusal to pay equal benefits for female and male civil servants. However, it is a step which the PAP government cannot retreat from because failure to consult obvious groups on actions that are prejudicial to them could well cause further erosion of electoral support, if the actions were not satisfactorily, normatively justified.

Third is the institutionalization of an independent press. A pro-government press is not synonymous with pro-consensus and national interests. That incumbent leadership may be more keen in retaining power than furthering collective interests is an ever present possibility. That is why constitutional changes to protect national reserves and ensure minority parliamentary representation are put in place by the government, notwithstanding hitherto clean leadership.

Contrary opinions do not disappear by their absence in the press; instead they bide their time for the opportunity to exercise their effect. Consequently, the lack of published information about contrary opinions renders the incumbent leadership unresponsive to opposition, including efforts to diffuse them, until their effects are manifested. Arguably, in 1991, the failure of the national press in this regard compounded failures of other feedback mechanisms to give the PAP an accurate reading of the electorate's sentiments, leading to a snap election that resulted in a further slide of popular support for the PAP.

The potential negative consequences demonstrate that an unquestioning pro-government press constitutes a monologue, rather than a conversation required for a strong consensus on national interests. Thus, pragmatically, communitarianism needs an independent press.

Conclusion

Recently, the political leadership in Singapore has come to define the difference between Singapore and Western capitalist societies as that of communitarianism versus individualism. Instead of questioning the accuracy of this characterization or speculating on the leadership's motive in doing so, the analysis essayed here takes the leadership's intention to develop a communitarian ideology seriously and suggests that the necessary conditions for a communitarian democracy have yet to be firmly established in Singapore, although the possibilities of such conditions developing are in place. Further political development will include, among other processes, increasing institutionalization of the rights to interest group formation and consultation, and a more independent press.

Trends, No. 40, *Business Times*, weekend edition, 25–26 December 1993

Debating ethnicity, welfarism, and population trends

chapter 7

Ethnic peace: a unique contribution

Raj Vasil

Nineteen-ninety constituted the most significant landmark in the political history of independent Singapore. Following a prolonged, even somewhat tedious, search by Mr Lee Kuan Yew for his political heir, he finally decided to bow to the human condition that governs our lives, dictated by the immutable process of change and renewal, and entrust the destiny of Singapore to his chosen successor.

The Singapore inherited by Prime Minister Goh Chok Tong and his colleagues is well-educated, prosperous, vibrant and enterprising. Above all, it is multi-racial and, based on the successful management of ethnicity by its first generation rulers, it has been remarkably free of any serious manifestations of ethnic rancour and conflict.

In today's context of vicious and savage world ethnic conflict, it must cause sobering reflection to contemplate what Singapore might have become but for the sagacity of its people and government. Undoubtedly, the key to the Singapore miracle has been the remarkably successful management of the country's ethnic diversity and, as such, today's multi-racial Singapore stands as the most monumental achievement of the People's Action Party (PAP). In this, the role of the people of Singapore should not be forgotten, for isn't there the oft-quoted saying that a people get the government they deserve?

It is not far-fetched to argue that without this critical achievement none of the other myriad components of the Singapore success story would have been possible; even the continued existence of Singapore as a sovereign state could not have been taken for granted.

Throughout the period leading to decolonization, conventional wisdom in Singapore had been that the country in terms of its location, population mix and entrepôt economy could survive and prosper only as a part of Malaya; only the foolhardy, including those given to Chinese chauvinism, could see any future at all for an independent Singapore. It was feared that in an independent Singapore, Chinese chauvinism and/or communism inevitably would gain such ascendancy that the country would virtually self-destruct. Thus, to start with, merger with Malaya was to override all other objectives and constitute the key to successful management of the "ethnic" question in Singapore.

Therefore, when in 1965 Singapore was forced to separate from Malaysia only two years after it had enthusiastically joined the new federation, it was genuinely mourned by the PAP as a disastrous misfortune. Announcing to his people on television the "mutual agreement" to separate, Mr Lee Kuan Yew was visibly overwhelmed by emotion.

However, the experience of that turbulent relationship with the Malay-dominated federal government in Kuala Lumpur had a positive side to it: it considerably reinforced the agenda of the PAP on the successful management of ethnicity in a fragmented society. Also, it psychologically prepared the people of Singapore, especially the Chinese majority, to willingly accept a genuinely multi-racial city-state.

The entire struggle that the PAP had waged while in Malaysia had been based on the notion of a multi-racial, Malaysian Malaysia in which, in the words of Mr Lee, "all its people, irrespective of their racial origins, enjoyed the good things of life on an equal basis".

It is one of those ironic twists of fate that two of its greatest assets, the location of Singapore in the middle of the Malay world of Southeast Asia and the ethnic mix of its population, also happen to constitute the greatest potential threats to its very existence and integrity. Located elsewhere, Singapore would easily have been viewed and accepted as a Chinese city-state, a Third China, based on the overwhelming preponderance of the Chinese in the population and their unmatched contribution to its progress and prosperity.

However, the political imperatives, at the time of Singapore's separation from Malaysia, were such that the Chineseness of Singapore had to be de-emphasized and the country presented to the world wrapped in multi-racial garb. Many in the Chinese community then viewed Singapore's independence as an opportunity for them to fully assume the reins of power in their own country and assert its Chineseness.

The critical task, thus, that the PAP had to face was to persuade the Chinese not to behave and act as a dominant majority and view Singapore as a Chinese city-state in which the Malay and Indian minorities were accorded only a subordinate role and status. It was no easy task, as at that time many Chinese viewed the assertion of their status as the dominant majority of Singapore as nothing other than their natural right.

From the beginning, the PAP's attempt to successfully manage Singapore's ethnic diversity took into account the country's socio-economic reality. They recognized that successful state-making had to have two critical components: one, an overall political and social environment that promoted ethnic contact and interaction, and two, rapid and continuing economic growth and prosperity.

Poverty, unemployment and illiteracy inevitably created a general environment of distrust, anger and unreasonableness that was given to cynical exploitation by opportunistic political leaders and organizations to foment ethnic confrontation and conflict.

It was thus imperative to the PAP that the success of their strategy for nationhood and the management of ethnicity had to depend substantially on continuing economic expansion and growth that ensured jobs, education and housing for all, and a reasonable standard of living. It was, further, correctly assumed that in a multi-racial society in which ethnicity still constituted the chief basis of political loyalty, a state that was founded on multi-racialism could secure and hold the loyalty and commitment of its citizenry only by guaranteeing a reasonably good life.

Paralleling this practical wisdom were the PAP's perceptions of ethnic assimilation and integration. Here, the PAP was fully convinced that assimilation or integration could not be ordered through legislation or political action. Recognizing that the different ethnic components of the Singapore population were likely to zealously guard their distinctiveness, the state had no choice but to adopt a broad-based ethnic agenda that did not conflict with the emotion-charged and critical issues of religion, culture, language and education espoused by various sections of the population.

Based on this, the central concept that the PAP leaders pursued was that Singapore would have to remain a multi-cultural, multi-lingual and multi-religious society for long, with each ethnic segment — the Chinese, the Malays, the Indians, and the others — enjoying autonomy and equality of status in their cultures, languages and religions.

Even though it had then been a widely accepted notion among the newly independent Third World states that for the sake of national unity and successful management of ethnicity, cultural, educational and linguistic diversity had to be reduced, if not altogether eliminated, the PAP rulers refused to be guided by that conventional wisdom. The absence of serious ethnic confrontation and conflict in Singapore during the last quarter century, while much of the rest of the world (including its neighbours in Southeast Asia) has been savaged by the viciousness of ethnic conflict and separateness, bears testimony to the success of the strategy of the first generation PAP leaders.

One wonders if, as the collective memory of the fateful experiences of the 1960s recedes, the new generations of Singaporeans and their leaders will be able to show the same special sensitivity displayed by those of the first generation. Will the present generation have the necessary predisposition and humility to recognize that in the management of ethnicity, one may not always be able to pursue and attain the rational and the ideal, and that there are inherent limits to what can be ordered and achieved through state manipulation and regulation? Will they be able to contain the temptation to extend their penchant for social engineering to the sphere of race relations and attempt to manage ethnicity through state regulation and action?

One can only hope that they will display the same patience shown by the first generation leadership and leave it, in the words of Mr Lee Kuan Yew, to "time and circumstance" to eventually create an entirely unified Singapore political community.

Trends, No. 4, *Straits Times*, 27 December 1990

chapter 8

An ethnically diverse nation's task

Ling Mei Lim

Singapore is coming into its own. But in its twenty-seventh year of independence, the quest to affirm what it means to be Singaporean still remains an important cultural agenda. The present economic stature of the whole Asia-Pacific seaboard has brought about the consciousness of a new momentum in Asian history, and with it a renewed zeal to embrace Asian roots. But on this uncertain terrain of defining cultural identity, a lot of muddy ink has been spilled.

A favourite shortcut is to identify cultural authentication with ethnic pride to see cultural affirmation solely as a matter of boosting ethnic Asian heritage. Behind this drive is a felt need to redress an imbalance that comes from an overzealous and indiscriminate mimicry of the West. There is a certain legitimacy to this.

What is more questionable is the attempt to justify this on the grounds that Asia's economic miracles are the sure expressions of the supremacy of Asian roots. Seen in this light, the emphasis on renewed ethnic pride comes like a form of self-congratulation. And self-applause spells complacency and stupor, not cultural vitality.

In the present context, we need to be reminded that cultural authenticity is a larger, more dynamic issue than that of ethnicity — the simple assertion of ethnic pride is not automatically or even necessarily culturally authenticating in its nature. However admirable it may be to deepen one's roots in one's ancestral culture, ethnic heritage is too narrow a basis for cultural development.

Moreover, it is a strategy that flies in the face of present realities, for the present economic emergence of the Pacific is not a purely Asian phenomenon: its roots and many dimensions of its manifestation are Western and dependent upon the West. It has a foot in both worlds, so that our present glory is not an argument for ethnic pride. It points, rather, to a cultural-historical complexity that is not taken fully into account because we have not really come to terms with it.

It is perhaps helpful and revealing to examine this issue from the linguistic angle, since language is a significant mark of a state of mind and cultural consciousness. Take the example of the Taiwanese writer, Lung Ying-tai, who is admired for her impeccable command of Mandarin. She lamented that her early respect and command of Mandarin caused her to despise and ignore the Taiwanese dialects around her, with the result that she never learnt her parents' dialects, and to this day is unable to curse in the earthy way native dialect speakers do. Instead, she is trapped in her learned elegances and the high manners of Mandarin, which were acquired almost entirely from books — a language whose native roots are in Beijing and, hence, a transplanted, almost artificial flower in Taiwan.

There is a clear parallel between Ying-tai's situation and that of many Singaporeans. If the loss of linguistic roots is a clear manifestation of the cultural rootlessness of the Western-educated Chinese who have abandoned their "native" culture to embrace the West, then it seems a simple corrective to diligently reapply oneself to the study of one's ancestral dialects. Yet, from another perspective, this could be as artificial to the present reality as the wholesale imitation of the West, for Chinese Singaporeans are the products of more complex historical and cultural forces than those which produced the dialects of their ancestors.

In fact, it can be argued that Singlish in the present historical context is more culturally authentic than ancestral dialects or even Tang poetry.

In her book, *Sons of the Yellow Emperor*, Lynn Pan mentioned language as a crucial test of one's "Chineseness". And for her, Tang poetry so embodies the quintessential Chinese sensibility that a Chinese without the linguistic ability to savour Tang poetry is cut off from what it feels to be Chinese at heart.

While this use of language and literature as an index of cultural sensibility may be useful, there is, perhaps, a more important lesson here. Language and literature are constantly evolving in relation to social-historical forces. Even if one could argue that Tang poetry is more quintessentially Chinese than any other writing in the whole of Chinese cultural history, the Chinese novelist today need not be castigated for not writing in Tang idiom and style. The modern Chinese novelist writes in the modern idiom, and he or she is not the less Chinese for doing so. To only mimic Tang Chinese at this point in history is to be false to the task of a twentieth century Chinese writer.

Lynn Pan herself is a lesson in this regard. She is multi-lingual and writes in both Chinese and English. Her fluency in both languages is admirable. She is a phenomenon that the Tang Dynasty neither witnessed nor produced. To say that her admiration and emotional sympathy for Tang poetry is a true index of her identity is an oversimplification of the case. She is wider and more complex than that. The whole cultural-historical situation of an "overseas" Chinese — educated in both English and Chinese, widely travelled and knowledgeable in both Western and Chinese cultures — better explains what she is than her love for Tang poetry. Here again, language serves as an important reference point: if bilingualism or multi-linguilism is considered a positive accomplishment and a key to an international arena, why cannot the same be said for cultural diversity within the soul of an Asian?

Southeast Asian Chinese are the products of international forces and should not try to be less than that. Cultural diversity is their roots and there are peculiar strengths which come with that. To begin exploring this perspective on cultural authenticity is to see at once that it is not a straightforward issue as ethnic recovery seems to suggest. Rather, there are paradoxical truths to come to terms with.

Singlish is one example of this in the linguistic realm. Through circumstances in history, the English language has become for most purposes the language of international communication. For Singaporeans who were taught English and who imbibed its accompanying cultural values at an early age, it was also true that they acquired them at a great cultural distance from their native sources and in an abstracted way — in the classroom and almost entirely from books.

Artificial as it may have been in the beginning, English has none the less provided Singaporeans today with an entrance into an international arena of ideas and communication which would not have been accessible in their native Chinese dialects.

While books, television and radio are abstract by the standards of native dialect roots, today these media shape profoundly the depths of one's consciousness and the world one lives in. They helped to create an international exchange of knowledge and ideas which have played a crucial role in the current economic emergence of Asia. They are, therefore, no less potent and vibrant for being abstract and "artificial".

In the final analysis, it would be false not to admit that there are corresponding wider gains in culture that in many cases outweigh that nagging sense of the loss of linguistic and ethnic roots.

As in the case of language and literature, the whole debate of cultural identity among overseas Chinese points to the inherent relativity and the limitations of the cultural categories they attach to themselves. Cultural identification is not the fixed, rooted thing it is taken to be. To identify it with biological heritage or with national origin is to see it too rigidly and narrowly, since cultural achievement is not a simple function of ethnic expression.

Culture is the result of the efforts of man to confront, understand and find ways of relating to the immensity and diversity within the universe. It concerns nothing less than his total effort to come to terms with the fullness of reality. Even though geographical and ethnic distinctions play a part, it is a human task which cuts across ethnic boundaries. At this point in history, it is increasingly clear that cultural development cannot remain merely regional because cultural fates are bound up with each other. Just as regional thinking alone is no longer sufficient for the economic reality of today, so there is a global dimension to the cultural task to which the mere assertion of ethnic pride would not suffice.

The new cultural pluralism of the international era calls for an active confrontation and testing of ideas which should be energizing and vitalizing to every culture involved. It is by testing differing ways of looking, feeling, thinking and doing that cultures keep vibrant and alive.

In this situation, the simple assertion of ethnic pride is a retreat from the scope and complexity of actively taking part in such an international dialogue. The gut-instinctiveness which one admires in the native (who appears not to have been traumatized by the wider implications of his or her culture) is, after all, not the best response in a complex international arena where finer and subtler delibera-tion of thoughts and values are called for.

For people at the crossroads of cultures as in Singapore and other overseas situations, ethnic allegiances have to be held at a certain tension and balance. It is this experience, of the relative tugs and pulls of differing cultural standards underlying one's daily existence, that puts Singaporeans in a unique advantage in a global situation. In the economic world, Singapore stands between the East and the West, so in culture the Singaporean has a unique opportunity to be a cultural link and bridge.

This calls for greater intellectual agility, not less. It is a greater, not a lesser, cultural vision; but to accept its challenge, one must see one's multi-ethnic background as a peculiar strength rather than a cultural weakness. A nation like Singapore, whose survival depends on remaining vitally engaged in the cross-cultural exchanges of our times, cannot sustain itself by mere ethnic pride. Instead, let Singaporeans not decline the unique advantages that the disparate social-historical forces of their overseas experience offer them. What they lose in "ethnic singularity", they more than make up for in versatility, cultural agility and communicative strength.

Trends, No. 28, *Business Times*, 31 December 1992

chapter 9

The paradox of ethnic-based self-help groups

Lily Zubaidah Rahim Ishak

When the Muslim self-help group, Mendaki, was established in 1982, few anticipated that it would be setting the scene for the birth of other ethnic-based, self-help organizations in Singapore. As Mendaki celebrates its tenth anniversary in 1992, some Singaporeans appear to be uneasy about how this trend towards ethnic-based approaches might adversely upset their nation's delicate multi-racial social fabric.

More Singaporeans are beginning to question whether the ethnic-based self-help paradigm undermines the multi-racial ideal upon which Singapore was founded. In adopting the ethnic-based self-help paradigm, are we unwittingly following in the footsteps of nations that have adopted ethnic-based communal initiatives in managing their multi-ethnic national composition?

To ensure that these concerns are resolved judiciously, greater public debate and discussion on the merits and demerits of the ethnic self-help approach is needed. Indeed, the safeguarding of multi-racialism as one of Singapore's most precious socio-political assets demands it.

Proponents of the ethnic-based self-help approach contend that it effectively harnesses the inherent potency of primordial ethnic sentiments. They assume that the socially privileged harbour stronger feelings of altruism and empathy towards their less well-off ethnic brethren, compared to others within the national community in a similarly disadvantaged position. Leaving aside the contentious moral and empirical dimensions of such claims, arguments based on the notion that primordial ethnic bias is a positive and immutable social given tend to promote feelings of insecurity and vulnerability amongst ethnic minorities.

These minorities may well fear that in times of political, social or economic instability, political leaders from the ethnic majority in government will fall prey to this primordial ethnic bias and orient policies accordingly. In a social milieu that is marked by ethnic insecurity, a combination of class and ethnic-based grievances may manifest itself in ethnic terms as the class dimension is effectively attenuated.

History is replete with examples of politicians and political parties in government and opposition resorting to forms of communal and other sectarian posturing for political gain, particularly when their political power is challenged, or tenuously held. If society is organized and mobilized on the basis of race, it can then be easily divided on the basis of race, rendering it easier for the various ethnic communities to be manipulated against one another on the basis of ethnicity. Multi-racialism thus becomes reduced to rhetorical sloganizing, whilst communalism cantankerously seeps into the social fabric of society as primordial clannishness is provided with a conducive environment.

The inherent weakness of the ethnic-based self-help paradigm in equitably assisting the academic underachievers and the underclass becomes particularly evident when the potent financial and resource base of the Chinese self-help group, Chinese Development Assistance Council (CDAC), is compared with those of Mendaki and Sinda (the Indian self-help group).

Even before its official inauguration on 20 September 1992, CDAC's endowment fund had accumulated an impressive sum of $5.5 million. Spurred on by the tremendous success of its fund-raising activities, it plans to raise a hefty $50 million in 10 years for its endowment fund alone. This ambitious target is more than likely to be realized as several multi-millionaire business magnates serve on CDAC's Board of Directors and as Trustees. In contrast to CDAC's impressive list of multi-millionaires, the Boards of Directors of both Mendaki and Sinda consist largely of civil servants, and community and grassroots activists whose material wealth is, by comparison, considerably less.

The generous financial incentives and awards of CDAC's Skills Upgrading Scheme appear to exemplify the unequal engines of support that are differentially rendered to the underachievers of each community via the disparate ethnic-based self-help bodies.

CDAC's generous incentives cannot easily be matched by Mendaki or Sinda due to their less robust financial resource base. For example, Chinese unskilled and semi-skilled workers are more likely to attain better qualifications and, thus, greater possibilities for social mobility than non-Chinese workers.

This, then, begs the question of whether it is fair that some members of the national community, because of their ethnicity, are provided with superior forms of assistance and are thus likely to emerge with a headstart in the "underachievers' race" for upward social mobility? With its larger population and stronger financial base, CDAC will thus not only be able to effectively sustain — but is also likely to widen — the Chinese community's already advantaged aggregate socio-economic and educational position relative to the other ethnic communities.

Instead of duplicating educational and other skills improvement programmes, there is a strong case to be made for the various self-help bodies — in a spirit of *gotong royong* co-operation, inter-ethnic goodwill and plain economic logic — to collectively harness their resources in joint programmes geared towards helping all socially disadvantaged Singaporeans.

Such inter-ethnic initiatives will not only help to break down pernicious ethnic stereotyping but also highlight the similar educational problems and social symptoms which beset the socially disadvantaged from all ethnic communities.

Various studies have indicated that the underclass and academic underachievers, regardless of their ethnicity, tend to have a low sense of self-esteem and often give up trying to persevere after repeated failures in school. Factors such as poor proficiency in English and limited parental supervision, and the lack of cultural and material capital, contribute significantly to their dismal academic progress compared to those students who are fortuitously well-equipped. If the underlying problem of academic underachievement is strongly class- rather than ethnic-based, it then logically follows that the focus on ethnic-based solutions needs to be reappraised.

The inherent contradictions and attendant inequities stemming from the ethnic-based self-help approach can be more clearly exemplified by drawing a parallel at the global level. If richer European nations only assisted less wealthy European nations and "richer" African nations were expected to help other poverty and famine-stricken African nations, inter-ethnic understanding and empathy at the global level would forever remain an unattainable utopian dream.

Over-reliance on sectarian ethnic-based approaches, whether at the villlage, national or global levels, tenaciously undermines social cohesion and the interaction of people across ethnic boundaries primarily as human beings, whilst promoting a sense of group separateness, competition and insecurity.

One is reminded of an old adage: the means of attaining a goal should be accorded the same priority as the ends used. This rationale rests on the understanding of the symbiotic linkage between the means and ends used and the damaging long-term ramifications of using the wrong means to achieve the right ends. As Mendaki celebrates its tenth anniversary and CDAC celebrates its formal inauguration, it may be timely for Singaporeans to reflect on the propriety of adopting ethnic-based self-help means if the multi-racial ideal is to remain unadulterated.

Trends, No. 25, *Business Times*, 24 September 1992

chapter **10**

Welfarism and an affluent Singapore

Liew Kim Siong

The inauguration of the Chinese Development Assistance Council (CDAC), together with other ethnic-based self-help organizations like Mendaki and Sinda, are part of the Singapore Government's new "many helping hands" approach aimed at creating "a more caring and compassionate society". While some critics charge that this way of helping the poor is divisive, others see such a communitarian welfare strategy as well-intended to bind the nation closer together through mutual help-giving. Whatever the views, events since the announcement of the government's paradoxical policy for "levelling up" society suggest the emerging significance of the welfare question in *The Next Lap* of Singapore's development.

Specifically, the outcome of the 1991 general election, where the PAP suffered a net loss of three parliamentary seats and a further slippage in its share of the popular vote, is an indication that the current management of the welfare question has become problematic. The issues that mattered most to voters were "bread and butter" ones, like the rising cost of living and doing business — summed up by the commotion over "the middle-class squeeze".

Moreover, as pointed out by the Editor of the *Straits Times*, the PAP was seen as "a greedy government", and voters were unconvinced that the public sector's preoccupation with accumulating surpluses benefited the average citizen. Thus, while it is generally true that incomes have risen, the bone of contention is whether hardworking citizens feel that they are getting back their "fair share".

Basis of political legitimacy

In the modern age, the political legitimacy of governments depends on how well they manage the welfare question to create economic growth and deliver a "fair share" to every citizen, thereby sustaining the social pre-conditions for the accumulation process in capitalism.

In Singapore, economic development has resulted in a visible and widespread uplifting of living standards, transforming a society that, hitherto, made do with survival and squalor into a society increasingly consumed with the trappings of affluence. The PAP government must be credited with having successfully managed the welfare question by generating rapid growth, while maintaining social cohesion and stability.

From the start, the priority, as outlined by a member of the PAP old guard, Dr Goh Keng Swee, was "... the accumulation of wealth through economic growth, rather than a more equal distribution of existing wealth and a proliferation of state welfare services".

Initially, however, economic development required "redistribution before growth", with massive investments in the social infrastructure, especially through heavily subsidized programmes in public housing, expanded education and improved health care. Such provisions in collective consumption goods constitute, in effect, welfare payments to the working class in order to incorporate them into the industrializing process. Without proper housing, education and health care, there would not be a motivated, disciplined and skilled workforce — currently ranked the world's best by one international business analysis firm — to attract much needed foreign investments.

Ideologically, the PAP's staunch rejection of state welfarism is the hallmark of a successful management philosophy that entails suppressing the articulation of welfare rights, which is central to the definition of modern welfare states. A sharp distinction is imposed between the provision of collective consumption goods as investments in the social infrastructure to support economic development, and "social welfare" as in the form of transfers in cash and services to a stringently tested underclass. This ideological strategy thwarts expectations for state subsidies as a right of citizenship and enforces an ethic of self-reliance.

But the welfare strategy that has "worked" thus far may now be subverted by the onset of affluence. Irresistibly, people's expectations rise according to the wealth of the nation. The current upgrading exercise for public housing estates, which goes beyond meeting the basic need for shelter, concedes to the political expediency in satisfying changing expectations in the quality of life, and implicitly acknowledges the real problem of relative deprivation.

In fact, the PAP government's "levelling up" policy, announced just before the polls in August 1991, admits that there are gaps in society. The danger here, as Senior Minister Lee Kuan Yew warned, is that:

> If we are to remain a socially mobile society, with no class distinctions or class hatreds, those who have risen up through meritocracy must take an active interest in the welfare and well-being of the less fortunate. Not to do so is to risk a gradual stratification of Singapore society. Then, the less successful will begin to resent those who are successful but do not bother about them.

Yet, exactly how "levelling up" can be achieved is not made clear. Even with billion dollar schemes, like Edusave, to maximize the potential of Singaporean children, and Medifund to help the poor pay hospital bills, which the government insists are "not entitlements", the basic idea to help people help themselves remains unchanged. Meanwhile, the efficiencies of the free market approach are re-embraced to justify the government's privatization plans, which caused much public alarm in the "restructuring" of government hospitals and the creation of independent schools.

Class cleavages

As class cleavages become more obvious and less tolerable, the fundamental question is whether the government's communitarian welfare strategy can forestall the emergence of class contradictions inherent with the development of a capitalist economy. The salience of class can be glimpsed from the nascent desire for a relationship between citizen and state, based less on sacrifice for economic goals but more on an equitable distribution of income and opportunities.

This is at odds with the PAP government's idea of welfare provisions as "privileges" doled out at the discretion of a paternalistic government that expects gratitude from the citizenry.

Ultimately, what is at stake is the cohesion and stability of society, which inevitably affects the performance of the economy. Thus, the welfare question will dominate the next stage of Singapore's development, as the citizens of this got-rich-quick nation try to imagine a sense of community.

Trends, No. 22, *Business Times*, 25 June 1992

chapter 11

A declining birthrate

Liak Teng Kiat

A National Day rally speech by Mr Lee Kuan Yew nearly 11 years ago signalled the start of Singapore's present population policy. In his speech, the then Prime Minister lamented what he called the "unintended consequences" of policy changes his government had made in the early years of its rule, in particular the introduction of universal education, provision of equal employment opportunities for women and the banning of polygamy, except for Muslims. At the time, he said, these measures "were manifestly right, enlightened and the way forward to the future". But they had also triggered changes the government had not foreseen that would cause Singapore's decline if not corrected.

Citing figures from the 1980 census, Mr Lee noted that as women acquired more education, they were less likely to get married. And those who did marry had fewer children than their less-educated sisters. This "lopsided" pattern of reproduction had profound implications for Singapore. If it continued, "we will be unable to maintain our present standards. Levels of competence will decline.

Our economy will falter, the administration will suffer and society will decline."

It was too late to reverse gear and have Singapore women "go back to their primary roles as mothers, creators and protectors of the next generation," Mr Lee added. "Our women will not stand for it. And anyway, they have already become too important a factor in the economy." All the government could do was to provide encouragement and incentives to better-educated women to have more children — a course he conceded might not work, going by the failure of incentives in Europe.

He was right, judging by the information now available. In the years since his speech, the government has introduced a host of fiscal and other measures to encourage marriage and motherhood, especially among the better-educated. These include match-making services, tax incentives, increased childcare facilities and easier access to foreign maids to ease the burdens of combining motherhood with career. But while the measures have produced results in individual cases, they do not appear to have had a significant impact at macro level so far.

Educationally, women have continued to advance. Among the 25–29 year age group, the proportion with upper secondary qualifications nearly doubled, to 12.2 per cent in 1990, while those with tertiary education nearly trebled, to 8 per cent (the corresponding figures for men were 13.2 per cent and 8.5 per cent respectively). This educational progress was accompanied by a rise in the numbers not married. Among those aged 25 and above with at least secondary education, the figure more than tripled between 1980 and 1990.

Overall, of course, marriage remained the preferred state among the vast majority, with only 8.3 per cent of 35-year-olds and above still single in 1990 (compared to 9.8 per cent for males). But increasingly, couples were opting for childless marriages despite publicity campaigns on the joys of parenthood. The proportion of all ever-married women with no children rose a third, to 12 per cent, in 1990. Among 25–29 year olds, the increase was from 19.2 to 33.6 per cent; among 30–34 year olds, from 6.9 to 14.4 per cent; and among the 35–39 age group, from 2.9 to 7.5 per cent.

Correspondingly, there has been a drop in the average number of children per ever-married women, from 3.4 to 2.9 per cent. As Mr Lee predicted in 1983, the government has had more success persuading the less-educated to have fewer babies than in encouraging the better-educated to have more. While the least-educated were having fewer babies, so too were those with more schooling. Indeed, whereas only women with tertiary education averaged fewer than two babies in 1980, by 1990, this was true also for secondary and upper secondary women.

In the short term at least, the education of women has been a boon to the economy. During a decade which saw the male labour participation rate fall in almost all age groups, that by women climbed five percentage points overall, to more than 51 per cent in 1992. Women now make up nearly two-fifths the entire workforce, accounting for close to three-quarters of all clerical workers, two-fifths the professional and technical workers, almost the same proportion of sales and service personnel and more than a third of all production and related workers. The only category where women have a relatively insignificant role is the administrative/managerial one where they hold less than a fifth of total positions.

But if Singapore's female labour participation rate is high among developing and newly-industrialized countries, and is comparable to that for industrial nations, it is not high enough for a country with persistent labour shortages. As economists have pointed out, more than half of all married women — most of them under 40 and educated; about half having at least secondary qualifications — are not in the labour force who could be employed usefully. They could, theoretically, replace a good portion of the more than 200,000 foreign workers now deployed in the economy.

The question is how to draw these women into the labour force — and whether it is desirable to do so. The answer to the first seems simple enough, on paper at least. Since most married women who drop out of the workforce do so to look after children, the way to attract them back is either through part-time employment, which would allow them to work without unduly neglecting their families, or provide even more home and childcare help than now available. A report on dual-career couples released in March by the Statistics Department is pertinent here. It notes a high correlation between the presence of a maid and children among dual-career couples, who now make up two-fifths of all married couples. Among the under-35s with a maid at home, only 4 per cent were childless and 84 per cent had children under five. For those without maids, 32 per cent were childless and only 52 per cent had children under five.

In practice, however, neither option looks ideal or even, in the case of part-time work, achievable in the near future. Despite official efforts to persuade employers to expand part-time work to accommodate mothers, the relatively easy availability of foreign workers has kept them resistant to change, unlike employers in industrialized countries. Tightening the supply of foreign workers could make them more amenable — but it could as easily drive up Singapore's already high cost of doing business and drive investors abroad where labour is still readily available. The provision of greatly expanded childcare facilities and further easing of rules on foreign maids can be accomplished more easily. Whether it is desirable is debatable. While the measures might be welcomed by many and would enable large numbers of mothers to work outside home, their impact on family ties are likely to be less than benign. At the very least, it is unknown territory to be entered only with a great deal of caution if Singapore is not to have a future Prime Minister expressing regret 10, 20 years hence, of the serious unintended consequences of having had the majority of today's children under the care of strangers during their formative years.

What, then, is the answer to the declining birthrate and shortage of talent? The government has obviously concluded that the most promising solution is immigration. In July 1989, following a crisis of confidence in Hong Kong in the wake of the Tiananmen incident in Beijing, it relaxed immigration rules to allow permanent residence not just to graduates and professionals but to craftsmen, technicians and experienced white-collar workers as well. Although this policy represented a major liberalization for Singapore, it was hardly novel. Countries like the United States, Canada and Australia had also concluded, years before, that the answer to the problem of falling birthrates was immigration. While these countries, unlike Singapore, give automatic priority to relatives of residents and citizens, would-be immigrants with the skills needed by the economies are also sought after.

There is, of course, a difference in scale between Singapore and these countries, both in terms of geographic size and population, which makes immigrants loom far larger for Singapore. And this gives the issue special sensitivity, as was evident in the immediate public reaction to the change of rules and the expected admission of large numbers of Hongkongers here. Opposition politicians claimed that immigrants would "steal" skilled jobs from Singaporeans while many workers, apparently, worried that immigrants would depress their wages.

Newspaper readers complained that the immigrants would aggravate the "rat-race", upset the country's racial balance or be unable to blend smoothly into Singapore's unique racial and cultural mix. There were grumbles too from some armed forces reservists about "giving" foreigners benefits they had not paid for by way of national service.

That the complaints have not resurfaced since, at least publicly, could mean that Singaporeans now accept the policy — or merely that it has not affected their lives in the way they feared it would since the still-buoyant economy has been able to absorb the newcomers without hiccup. But the experience in Western countries where hostility to immigrants has grown as their economies declined indicates that this apparent acquiescence could disappear in the event of an economic downturn.

What has happened in the West is not simply a case of racism, although it appears that way because Asians and other non-whites have been the main targets of resentment. In Germany, for example, many regard ethnic Germans from the former Soviet Union as unwelcome aliens. Indeed, grumbles may be heard among those in the former West Germany of those from the East — and vice versa. So the fact that approved immigrants to Singapore will be mainly of Chinese, Indian or Malay stock, in order to maintain the present racial balance, is no guarantee of their continuing acceptability to locals. It might be noted that the majority of those who originally objected to Hongkongers being admitted in large numbers as migrants into Singapore were fellow ethnic Chinese.

None the less, the dangers of not doing anything outweighs the risks of any public unhappiness over immigration. In the absence of any more viable solution to the problem of declining birthrates and its implications, not just for the economy but also national security because there will be fewer young men available for national service, Singapore has no alternative but to bring in outsiders to make up for its shortfalls in labour and talent. The problem, in fact, may not be too many immigrants but too few. Although impressive numbers have been granted permanent residence in recent years — more than 20,000 a year between 1990 to 1992, three times the figure for 1983 and 1984 — rather fewer have actually settled in Singapore. And if the Western economies recover dramatically, those who now opt for Singapore for want of other choices may decide that the bigger countries would afford them better opportunities.

But even in the best-case scenario, immigration addresses only one aspect of Singapore's demographic woes. It can only make up for the missing numbers resulting from fewer babies. It offers no solution to the less apparent, less measurable consequences of fewer babies, that is its long-term impact on family ties and family values. No one watching the United States and some other Western societies self-destruct now doubts the importance of the family for societal well-being. The challenge is how to prevent its erosion in small — and relatively affluent — families where children are far more likely to be indulged and pampered than taught sharing and responsibility. Ironically, these same children will have greater burdens to bear as their parents age and need support simply because they will have fewer, if any, siblings to share the responsibility with. And what of the adults who do not marry, or choose not to have children if they do?

That Singapore will go quite the way of the West is unlikely given the government's active campaign, supported by other opinion-makers, to preserve the family. But change will come, which is likely to place great pressure on future governments intent on preserving the present anti-welfarism policies. In theory, the aged of the future should be more financially secure and better able to look after themselves than today's old, having greater earning power and thus more savings to their credit. In practice, however, many are likely to find their savings inadequate, whether due to their own fecklessness or rising costs. Those with families can, like today's old, expect sustenance from them. But what of those — the growing numbers — who do not have families? Then as now, there will be calls for the state to step in. But unlike now, such demands are likely to be much harder to put off.

Trends, No. 44, *Business Times*, weekend edition, 30 April–1 May 1994

Aspects
of
Singaporeanness

chapter **12**

Comparing the Singaporean undergraduate with the American

Janadas Devan

How good a student is the Singaporean undergraduate? Does the education system allow him to fulfil his full potential? A logical way of answering these questions is to compare the Singaporean with students from other systems. How well does Singapore's education system stack up, for instance, against that frequent source of admiration and blame, the American? Comparisons of this kind, however, frequently descend into cliché. Most distinctions made between American students (who are popularly acknowledged as articulate, critical, independent) and Singaporean students (who are almost always described as hardworking but passive and dull) mistake appearances for truths.

There are undoubtedly differences between the two student populations, and it will profit us to understand their exact nature. But after six years of undergraduate teaching in the humanities at a well-regarded American university and before that, at Singapore universities — I would hesitate to use terms like "independent" and "dull" to describe the differences, which are a good deal more complex than these terms allow.

What is not commonly realized, for instance, is that though American students are generally more articulate than their Asian counterparts, they are also as intellectually conservative. As accepting of the ethos of their society as Singaporeans are supposed to be of ours, they are equally products of a culture skilled at encouraging ideological conformity. Interestingly, the nature of the American classroom hinders the recognition of that conservatism. The presence of debate, the lively atmosphere of the classroom, can mask the absence of genuine inquiry, as students expend a good deal of time and energy arriving at conclusions they already hold.

But one should not discount the pedagogical usefulness of an educational culture that places a premium on debate. Even if that debate has more form than substance, nothing prompts greater clarity in teaching than the effort to respond to challenging or dissenting questions. And nothing is more helpful to a student than an atmosphere that allows the asking of any question, without fear of embarrassment, ridicule or rebuke.

But the commendable openness of discussion in the American classroom does not in itself guarantee excellence. Indeed, as I was repeatedly surprised to discover, my students, in fact, knew very little. As surprising as this may sound, the average American undergraduate at a major university is probably less knowledgeable in a given field of learning than his average Singaporean counterpart. Though I am generalizing from my own experience, this impression is confirmed by numerous recent reports on the deteriorating state of American education at all levels below the postgraduate.

What is puzzling, however — and this is the real paradox of the U.S. system — is that though the average undergraduate disappoints, the very best are incomparable. For every sixty students I taught each year, there would be at least one of astonishing ability, so far outstripping his, or her, peers in brilliance as to seem to come from an altogether different universe.

I believe it is this gap — the shocking difference — between the average and the superlative, and not liveliness or independence of mind, that distinguishes the American undergraduate from the

Singaporean. That gap, I am convinced, is narrower among Singapore's undergraduates than among America's.

How does a system that seems to generate a low average produce individuals that are so exceptional? And why does a system like ours, that manages a better average, fail to produce incomparable talents as often as the high average might lead one to expect?

The usual clichés come to mind. Our students belong to a cultural milieu that emphasizes training and skills acquisition, but not intellectual growth. American culture, while neglecting the average, celebrates individualism and the exceptional individual, who consequently thrives. So goes the usual refrain.

Another explanation is statistical: in a population of more than 250 million people, however mediocre the general standard of education, nature, with the help of judiciously applied immigration laws, is generous enough to cast up individuals who rise dramatically above the rest.

This is not, however, a sufficient explanation. Firstly, though nature is parsimonious in disposing its gifts upon a society, it usually maintains the proportions of what statisticians call a "normal curve". It does not, while conferring upon one particular soul all seven graces in abundance, confer upon 10,000 others only a single, paltry one. The difference between the average and the superlative among my students was just too immense for the laws of probability to hold sovereign sway.

Secondly, I know of a number of average or above-average students from Singapore who, transplanted into an American university, turn into fine academic swans. Without losing their disciplined habits, they become adventurous, confident, and intellectually expansive.

The experience of these Singaporeans overseas suggests that the explanation rests, not in culture or genetics, but in the different educational systems. What the Singapore system achieves is the maintenance of a high average by applying a constant pressure that forces students to meet established common standards. At periodic intervals in the student's life, he must cross formidable hurdles in the form of mass examinations before proceeding to the next stage.

By the time the average student arrives at the university, he has already successfully negotiated a slew of stringent examinations. Augmenting the traditional investment in education, this continually applied external pressure ensures that the average undergraduate can excel academically, even when institutions or teachers are flawed.

Nothing comparable to this pressure exists in the United States. Lacking a set of universally applied standards, schools in various parts of the country find their own levels. Though the woes that afflict the American education system have multiple causes, the absence of such a standard has helped worsen the problems. Only recently have educationists begun to discuss the creation of a national standard to provide incentives for students and teachers alike to do better than the prevailing lowest common denominator. Students, thus, typically arrive at major universities undeserving of the excellence of their institutions.

Yet, it is precisely this lack of a standard process and a fixed structure that has enabled the unusual American student to soar much above the level of his peers. I can best illustrate this paradox by describing an encounter with such a student three years ago.

He was an extraordinary young man of sixteen in his first year of undergraduate study. After a few weeks of classes, it became clear that the only way I could adequately teach this student was to conduct another seminar outside class, with a different syllabus, just for him. By the end of the semester, I had to involve my colleagues in his work because he had begun to examine issues which were not altogether familiar to me.

At semester's end, Andrew wrote a term paper the quality of which was staggering. A few months after its submission, I read a scholarly article by a senior professor, published in the most prestigious journal of my discipline, on the same subject as Andrew's paper. The article was lengthy and erudite, skilfully deploying the familiar apparatus of critical scholarship. Astonishingly, Andrew's paper had anticipated everything the senior professor had to say.

Remarkable as this student was, his wonderful essays could not have been conceived without extra-curricular nurturing. He was helped ungrudgingly; everyone was eager to teach him; nobody, including his peers, complained. In an educational system like Singapore's, such help and attention as he received might have been thought unfair. A system where all students are assessed by a uniform set of criteria involving common examinations tends to produce an over-investment in a level playing field.

Within a year, Andrew was admitted to what is known as the Honours students programme, which allows him to bypass set requirements. In close consultation with academic advisers he himself selected, he put together a programme of his own devising that crossed disciplinary boundaries. He attended graduate courses if he found them interesting, or did reading courses specially tailored for him by individual professors. An enormous freedom — nurturing both discipline and romance — was granted him to pursue interests that were truly his own. These were extraordinary privileges.

A point I have put aside till now is that the flexibility of the U.S. system — the absence of a standard process and a fixed structure — allows not only geniuses to thrive. At the level of undergraduate education, the same flexibility that permitted Andrew to work at his own pace and talents also allows students who are slow learners, late developers — indeed, all kinds of other students — similarly to proceed at their own pace, nurturing their particular abilities through diverse combinations and types of courses.

A student who is not in an Honours programme retains the possibility of graduating with full honours and distinctions at the end of his studies, without penalty, in whatever period of time seems reasonable.

The Singapore system can profit from this flexibility without paying for it by the loss of standards. The way a general decline of standards has blighted the lives of countless young people in the United States is nothing less than criminal. Obviously, we cannot afford to relax standards that have served the majority of Singaporean students well. It is equally obvious, however, that the Andrews of this world cannot be processed according to fixed structures.

chapter 13

Kiasuism and the withering away of Singaporean creativity

David Chan Kum Wah

Kiasuism has been an issue in the press recently. Is it a Singaporean trait? Should we fight it or accept it? There is no denying that the behaviour of many Singaporeans is characterized by *kiasuism*. But the more important questions have not been examined yet: what makes people *kiasu*? How does *kiasuism* affect Singapore's future?

To be *kiasu* is literally to be afraid to lose out. As Mr Kiasu, a local cartoon character, would put it, "Better grab first, later no more." In other words, play it safe. Take whatever you can secure even if you are not sure whether you really want it. This is considered preferable to waiting for something better to come along. A bird in hand is worth any number in the bush. Another hallmark of *kiasuism* is conformity. If somebody else wants something, it must be good. Why take the risk of missing out on something others are enjoying? The result is a herd mentality where everyone goes after the same things and avoids the same things. No one wants to be different. To understand why people in Singapore are *kiasu*, I want to compare Mr Kiasu with Baron Munchausen, a character from legend whom

Singaporeans may have seen in a film shown on television. In the film, the Baron is in a town besieged by Turks in the Middle Ages.

In a theatre, the Baron tells his fantastic story of how he defeats the Turks with the help of his few extraordinary assistants. Pitted against the Baron is the Town Councillor, who is the voice of reason and has little tolerance for such artistic excesses. To him, the Baron is a subversive influence who distracts the people from the urgent task of confronting the Turks. The Baron is a dreamer whose sense of reality differs from that of his opponent. His imagination stretches reality beyond what reason holds to be possible. At the end of his story, the Baron challenges the townspeople to make his story real. "Open the gates," he says. "The Turks are still there," argues the voice of reason.

What would Mr Kiasu do? Why take such risks? Let's huddle behind our protective walls, even if it means that the siege continues. Better this than stepping out into the great unknown beyond.

I think some readers will see immediately the analogy for Singapore. For another hot issue in the press is that of building up an external economy. How are we to overcome the reluctance of Singaporeans to give up the security of life at home to venture abroad?

It has been suggested that the solution is to make life less secure in Singapore. The government has been providing too many safety nets: good public housing, transportation, education and health care. Is this wrong? The problem is rather that Singaporeans are averse to taking risks, which boils down to plain *kiasuism*. So a better solution would be to change the *kiasu* attitude.

To do that, we must understand the causes of *kiasuism*. Again, Baron Munchausen can help us here. As I said, the Baron is a dreamer whose fertile imagination breaks through the mental barriers of reason. I remember a survey published in the *Straits Times* a few years ago which found that most young Singaporeans did not have any big dreams. They mentioned a piece of property, a car and security in a well-paying job, when asked to name their aspirations in life.

Something in our society has conspired to drain away the

imagination of our youth. At an early age, they are already pragmatic and realistic. They are not idealists who want to change the world. Instead of striking out on their own paths, they follow in the footsteps of those who have gone before them. Their role models are rich bankers, lawyers and doctors.

Why is it that our young people are so conventional and unimaginative? Our education system has the greatest impact on our youth. It is a stifling system that has the narrowly-defined goal of producing students who do well in exams. It values the end-result and not the process of education. It is an unforgiving system that does not offer second chances for those who fail at any of its hurdles.

This is a system that teaches our young not to take risks. Choose the subjects that you can do well in and that will maximize your chances for a good job. Do not read anything out of your own interest and do not try to show initiative. Study past-year questions and model answers, and regurgitate them as best as you can. The more creative of Singaporean youth either fall by the wayside or learn quickly what matters.

Singapore's education system reflects society at large. Students grow up to view life on the same model: don't be different for there are no second chances if you fall. Life is the same rat race as school. It is every man for himself and we must compete or fall behind. Those who do not make it are given little compassion for they are just not good enough to survive in the Darwinian marketplace. We are told not to trust those who advocate a slower pace of life. Such negative thinking will hurt our competitiveness.

Lack of imagination and *kiasuism* are connected because the latter results from too many people placing too much value on the same narrow set of goods for which they all compete. Why are people so *kiasu* as to queue up overnight to buy a condomonium unit, and to bid high for their Certificates of Entitlement (COE) for cars? Because their whole purpose in life is tied up in that private property and that new car. There is little else that they can find fulfilment in. There is no alternative lifestyle that would satisfy them. How can they not want those material goods that everyone else covets?

Imagine now what someone could lose if he ventures into a new direction. If he gives up a secure job, he cannot immediately buy that property or car which will cost even more in the future. If he goes overseas, his children will miss out on places in the best schools at home. Can he take the ridicule he may face for doing something different? Can he be satisfied with the allure of adventure or the satisfaction of doing something for his own self-fulfilment?

The pressure to conform and to participate in materialistic pre-occupations is so strong in Singapore that even those who are aware of the possibility of alternative pursuits find themselves drawn into the rat-race. And the competitive mindset is so endemic that it manifests itself in the most trivial matters. The way Singaporeans rush to get on a bus or train makes it look like there is a prize for being first, and that getting a seat is the ultimate triumph in life. And somehow it is worth sacrificing an hour of your time to get something worth a few bucks which you may not really want, as long as it is free.

Every now and then, we find *kiasuism* becoming an obstacle to some objective of the state. Unfortunately, this is not seen as reason for changing the values of Singapore society. Instead, *kiasuism* is used to persuade people to achieve economic and social objectives. If people are too *kiasu* to work abroad, then we must convince them that it is materially rewarding to do so. They are offered state support to ameliorate the risks, and new role models of entrepreneurship are held up for emulation. People are told not to miss opportunities for making money. The state's goals can be achieved in this way but, in the process, *kiasuism* is being reinforced.

It is far better in the long run to address the root causes of *kiasuism*. For that is the only way to nurture people with compassion, vision and creativity, and to retain such people in Singapore. It is also the only way to reduce state intervention in the lives of people, for there would be less need for the kind of manipulation of *kiasuism* described here in order to achieve socially desirable goals.

If the cause of *kiasuism* is an education system that stifles the imagination and snuffs out the dreams of our youth, then we need a more liberal education system which allows children to develop in their own directions and which recognizes achievements not reflected in rigorous examinations. We also need society to become more tolerant and appreciative of creative talent and alternative lifestyles. We must show children that it is possible to fulfil other dreams in Singapore besides that of material well-being.

Such changes are a lot to ask of those in Singapore who have a vested interest in the present value-system and social structures. Ultimately, what is at issue is the kind of society we want to live in. Technology and economic development have brought Singaporeans material success. But do we want our lives to be governed by the demands of economics? Do we want our destinies to be determined by cost-benefit analyses and feasibility studies? Or do we want to cultivate our capacities for imagining new possibilities and fulfilling our dreams without being held back by pragmatism?

A life where one is free to dream is a more fulfilling one. But tolerance of the non-conformist is hardly the norm in Singapore. Ironically and symptomatically, the telecast of the film on Baron Munchausen was censored. What was cut out? The scene of Venus emerging from the giant shell, which was actually based on a masterpiece, The Birth of Venus, by the Italian Renaissance painter Botticelli. So who can dream of being an artist in Singapore? It is because people have given up hope of pursuing non-conventional alternatives in Singapore that they have stopped dreaming.

Trends, No. 34, *Business Times*, weekend edition, 26–27 June 1993

chapter 14

Frugality jockeys with conspicuous consumption

P. Lim Pui Huen

It is often said that it is the age-old virtues of industry and frugality of their pioneering forefathers that built up the thriving prosperity that Singaporeans enjoy today. Indeed, the coolie toiling in the hot sun, carefully hoarding his meagre pennies, is one image Singaporeans carry of their past. But what of these virtues today? Do they still exist and are they still relevant?

Firstly, as to industry, many visitors from more leisurely societies have commented that Singaporeans work too hard. So much pressure, they say, and no five-day week. The use of words too has changed. Hard work of the kind that means back-breaking labour is, thankfully, a thing of the past. So are the sweat shops of the 1950s and 1960s. Singapore workers are among the highest paid in Asia. Nowadays, the keywords are productivity and competitiveness. That is to say, people work hard but with intelligence and with enhanced skills. Working hard but playing hard can be compatible with the good life and with economic growth.

But frugality? A walk down Orchard Road will quickly put that idea out of anyone's mind. Consumerism is honoured in the name of trade, and the size of the retail trade in Singapore's economy is not to be discounted. Barely having recovered from Christmas, Singaporeans find the Lunar New Year upon them. Shops quickly put away the artificial snow and replace it with artificial fire-crackers. If Christmas is a marketing strategy, so is the Lunar New Year, only differently packaged.

Moreover, frugality is, frankly speaking, a function of necessity. People as a rule do not enjoy penny-pinching and making do. But the immigrant coolie who was paid $3 a month had no choice. What other options had he except to hold on to what little he had? Savings were an absolute necessity to provide minimum security for himself in an alien environment. Life was bare and basic, a matter of sub-sistence rather than living. But somehow, these coolies of bygone days survived and some even made good. Many well-known Chinese businesses started from grandfather's humble beginnings. From small savings, the process of capital accumulation began and, helped by ingenious methods of raising credit, the seeds of entrepreneurship grew. For, as scholars have pointed out, the Chinese peasant came from a society that knew how to handle money.

Nevertheless, one can only be pleased that standards of living have moved well beyond mere subsistence. Affluence has given people not only the freedom from want but also the freedom of choice. The average Singaporean no longer has to choose between doing without this or that, but rather, between having this or that.

It is a choice of lifestyle, and increasingly, the choices are being made. Take car ownership for example. In spite of exorbitant costs and official disincentives towards car ownership, the sale of cars continue to go up. Private apartments are still preferred although government housing is available at more affordable prices. A drive around the residential areas will reveal that small houses are being renovated into splendid mansions. Club memberships requiring four-figure to five-figure entrance fees are eagerly snapped up. Flights out of Singapore during the Lunar New Year and other holidays are booked months in advance. Shopping centres are full of designer-label speciality shops and HDB (Housing Development Board) carparks full of Mercedes-Benzs.

Are these kinds of conspicuous consumption sustained by well-heeled expatriates and tourists? With the world in recession, they are fewer in number and less open-handed than before. But shops and restaurants are full of people. Are Singaporeans living beyond their means? Are they living on the never-never, or almost never-never, relying on the year-end salary bonus to bail them out? Or does the free spending come from a sense of security induced by a buoyant economy and a buoyant job market?

And yet, in spite of all this, Singapore has one of the highest rates of domestic savings in the world. Contributions to the CPF take about 20 per cent out of employees' salaries every month. The size of Singapore's reserves is the envy of many larger countries. It is no wonder that Singapore maintains a strong guard over its hard-earned reserves. The correlation between savings, investment and economic growth is well understood. In analysing the historical, economic and political factors that lie behind the rapid economic growth of the four Little Dragons, Ezra Vogel pointed to the importance of "the habits of the heart", those attitudes, traditional institutions and values that are inherent in those societies. These include the work ethic, the ability to endure short-term hardship, and the achievement of high savings rates.

Saving for a rainy day is perhaps one of the deepest gut instincts of the Chinese, and a tolerance for delayed gratification is a lesson learnt over centuries of hardship and adversity. The lessons grandfather taught have not been entirely forgotten. But then, grandfather never knew the word "lifestyle".

Trends, No. 29, *Business Times*, weekend edition, 30–31 January 1993

chapter 15

Is Singlish becoming a language of prestige?

Lee Gek Ling

We English-educated Singaporean professionals in our 20s and 30s seem to slum it linguistically when we speak with each other. Yet, we don't do it when there is a foreigner or expatriate in our midst. This form of English need not be full-blown Singlish of the sort our low humour is made of, viz. Paik Choo and Siva Choy, but it is definitely less polished than what we would use in mixed company and, more importantly, recognizably local.

For example, we might say to a friend, "Aiyah, you!" instead of "Why are you so late?" The reply might be, "Sorry lah, no taxi", instead of "I'm sorry but there wasn't a taxi to be had".

This deliberate slumming is not necessarily derogatory towards the habitual speakers of the lowest form of Singapore English, but rather a familiarity marker and an act of identity. Anecdotal evidence includes a high-flying civil servant who says she uses a form of Singlish to narrow the chasm between herself and the company she's with. A legal service officer now in New England said it brought compatriots together and celebrated their distinction from WASPs and other in-sects. There are exceptions who claim they would never sink into such a linguistic abyss. However, trends are not concerned with the exceptions.

It has become "trendy" to slum it for two reasons — both due, in part, to a generation which went through their rebellious teen years against the backdrop of an academic debate over whether Singaporeans should speak proper English, and whether they should be allowed to lapse into the then-just-discovered creature "Singlish".

Schools, rules and daffodils

In the early 1970s, through to the mid-1980s, when those in the age range in question were in school, or just out of it, there was a conflict between language prescriptivists and the descriptivists. The former are those who prescribe grammar rules and standard English sentence structures as obligatory. By standard, they meant English as it is spoken by the Queen of England, or the BBC, or at least Raffles English, as spoken by Mr Lee Kuan Yew and that generation who had a sound grounding in grammar. Proponents included Lee Sow Ling, the language consultant and watch-dog of English used in the *Straits Times*, and Rebecca Mok, who designed a grammar-filled secondary English syllabus, and The Establishment.

Descriptivists believe that any form of a language is all right, as long as speaker and hearer comprehend each other. Their interest lies in describing the peculiarities of the form. Among these were various expatriate lecturers (how ironic): John Platt and his wife Heidi Webber, and the former Anthea Fraser Shields (now Gupta). Evidence of this conflict of "speak properly" versus "why don't you hang loose" resided not only in the academic papers churned out to lengthen publication lists, but also in a prolonged exchange of letters between the two camps in the Forum pages of the *Straits Times*, and various policy statements by the Ministry of Education on the kind of English that would be acceptable in schools and, where the nail that would shut the coffin of the dreadful spectre of Singlish was supposed to have been lethal, in examination scripts.

So, what does this have to do with the target group? I think that being in school then, and being taught that under no circumstance would Singlish be tolerated only made it all the more delectable, being forbidden fruit.

I am who I am

In conjunction with teen rebellion comes the need for a sense of identity. The 1970s and, especially the 1980s, saw the rise of nationalist propaganda to foster a Singaporean identity, from the wordy songs of the 1970s, which encompassed everything from the harbour being the fourth busiest port (then true), to our clean, green environment and tall white HDB (Housing Development Board) blocks to the infinitely more catchy "Stand up, Stand Up For Singapore" in 1986.

Le Page and Tabouret-Keller argue in their book *Acts of Identity* that how we speak can be a focus of who we are, a linguistic equivalent of "I speak, therefore I am", to parody Descartes. I think that the promotion of national identity and the teenage need for identity merged when the generation in their 20s and 30s adopted a less polished form of English as their norm among equals.

This need for a sense of identity is perhaps borne out in various public statements, from the oft-quoted (at least in sociolinguistic papers promoting Singlish) "And I should hope that when I am speaking abroad, my countrymen will have no trouble recognizing that I'm from Singapore" by Professor Tommy Koh, to the quote in an excellent article on Singapore humour by Ng Sek Chow and Eddie Guo of the Singapore International Foundation magazine *Singapore*, in which local comedian Jack Neo says, "We should be proud to be Singaporean in the way we speak". Whilst the context was Singapore Mandarin, I think extrapolations may be made to Singapore English.

Laugh and everyone laughs with you

How the use of a less polished form of English became trendy can be attributed, to some extent, to the tremendous popularity of a run of musical comedies by personalities such as Dick Lee, Michael Chiang and Jacintha Abishegenadan. The large audiences which paid to see The Chettiar's Daughter, Bumboat, and, more recently, Army Daze, Beauty World and Fried Rice Paradise, show that The Establishment's views on proper English are not held by everyone. The practitioners of these Singlish productions were in school in those conflict years and their use of Singlish may be a deliberate assertion of identity over Establishment views. Beauty World sold 8,788 tickets for eleven performances, and Fried Rice Paradise attracted 18,000 to its 20 performances. The immense drawing attraction of these TheatreWorks productions seems to be continuing, with 11,800 tickets sold as of 31 May 1992 for their latest offering, Michael Chiang's Private Parts.

Whilst a direct correlation cannot be made between audience figures and the rise of a form of Singlish as a familiarity marker, or act of identity, the numbers indicate a degree of popular awareness of the form. Presumably (because no pink identity cards were checked), the audience would have had a relatively stable percentage of the 20s to 30s age range of Singapore professionals.

The use of some form or other of Singlish also permeates other avenues of local humour, the books of Toh Paik Choo and Catherine Lim's O Singapore! Stories in Celebration, comedy tapes such as Siva Choy's "Why U So Like Dat?", and the political jokes which make the coffee shop rounds. It is found in other more serious fiction as pointed out by Ravi Veloo in a Straits Times article. The use of a variant linguistic form, even in humour, tends to make it more prestigious, and when something is more prestigious, more people would want to use it — which is the case here and now.

These are the reasons why I think we are "so like dat", and that it is a charming spontaneity. "Speak on, speak on for Singapore!"

chapter 16

Where gilded youth are lacking in heart

Derek da Cunha

Every man who will not have softening of the heart must at last have softening of the brain.
— G.K. Chesterton

It is said that most people are forever stamped by the culture of their adolescence. The ethos of the school in which they had been reared, in particular, represents an indelible marque which they will carry through much of life.

So, when young, if you had studied in a certain school with a reputation for turning out fashionable youth who are among the sons of Singapore's wealthiest families, chances are you will continue to affect the manner of the preppy youngster for many years to come. Yes, a charmed life of almost permanent adolescence amidst the very clubby atmosphere of the old boy network: a person with almost an obsessive preoccupation with form.

On the other hand, if you went to the "other place", which has always drawn some of the most intelligent boys from across Singapore's social spectrum, it is likely that you will forever be indebted to the system which gave you that leg up in life. And this would be translated into the figure of the deeply loyal, but colourless, servant of the state, who would not even think of rocking the boat. A man for whom one can have some admiration (for his achievements) but not warmth. Definitely not warmth.

Alternatively, like myself, you could have been schooled in a particular missionary tradition that emphasized almost a Franciscan-like approach to life. ("Learning how to live is more important than earning a living", the ever so slightly poetical headmaster of 20 years ago used to constantly remind us impressionable boys during assembly.) That being the case, you might have cultivated a penchant for easy moralizing, and more often than not find yourself embattled. In short, not exactly an individual given to sang-froid.

Generalizations, no less. And generalizations can prove hazardous. But there are rich veins of truth running through these particular generalizations; and the message they convey is that, for good or ill, we reap what we have sown.

Are we sowing the seeds of young Singaporeans who are spoilt? Apparently so. That, at least, is the view of Dr Albert Winsemius in an interview in the *Sunday Review* on 2 January 1994.

The one-time economic adviser to the Singapore Government is right. But he has captured only a small part of the picture of the young Singaporean that emerges in the 1990s. The broader canvas is even less flattering. In this, the last, decade of the twentieth century, we are seeing an individual's sense of social obligation, once stressed in the days of our parents' youth, slowly wither away. We are also seeing a newly-acquired complacency and self-satisfaction take root among the young. These traits are fast replacing traces of humanism, which in a past era had moved young Singaporeans to idealistic action.

Today, many among the young *élite* are hiding behind their pre-occupation to secure straight As and a wad of tertiary degrees to absolve themselves of social responsibility. It is the sort of pat, facile justification that merely confers a spurious dignity on the individual. Examples abound. One need only recall those smug students of a certain polytechnic who strenuously objected to the proposed siting near their campus of a hospice for the terminally ill. It was only the public uproar which followed that led these "solid citizens" of tomorrow to a change of heart. But too late; by their initial response they had secured their own condemnation.

A salutary example, but hardly an isolated one. Consider the report, "Some schools 'too busy' to join aid project for Somalis", which appeared in *The Sunday Times* on 6 June 1993. According to the report, when schools were approached to spend a single Sunday to help raise funds for starving Somalis, only 15 out of 150 schools responded in the affirmative. For most of the rest, the response was apparently "sorry, it is too time-consuming".

Too time-consuming to spend a single Sunday to help starving people, but evidently ample time to indulge in expensive, three-week jaunts to the idyllic rural fastnesses of Austria, Britain and Germany, and which has become almost *de rigueur* for some, *élite*, junior colleges. "It's hard-earned money. It means a lot to working-class people like us who don't have much to spare," intoned a Madam Helen Yap on these "educational" trips (*Straits Times*, 7 April 1992).

Gilded youth, part of a new *bourgeois-effete* crowd, who are largely lacking in humanism. It is a disturbing trend.

The reasons for the apparent absence of a humanistic spirit in many young Singaporeans are not entirely obscure. Perhaps one reason is that Singaporeans of all ages are fast losing a sense of tragedy in life that gives quality to thought and action. It is this very quality that provides depth and tone to the picture of intellectually rich and curious personalities, the sort ideally suited to assume the mantle of leadership as the nation strides towards its destiny in the twenty-first century.

Instead of such individuals, we are presented with a very different picture: people who have little awareness of issues outside their narrowly-defined fields of interest, and those who set great store by surface things, a dubious glamour, and a vacuous materialism so deftly stressed at all levels of society.

Amidst such a dismal picture, however, there are inspiring exceptions, such as that National University of Singapore under-graduate who demonstrated that a single, ordinary person can help raise the level of society's environmental consciousness; or that young, brilliant doctor, the recipient of the 1993 Lee Kuan Yew Scholarship, who decided to dedicate a part of himself to fund-raising work for the aged; or those young Singaporeans who took a year off their careers to work with the less fortunate in Third World countries under the Singapore Volunteers Overseas (SVO) programme.

These are noble Singaporeans; they manifest a lightness of soul and a self-denying nature.

Sadly, however, nobility, as a concept, cannot be taught — it must come from the heart, spontaneously. And this is the rub: though many of us appear to have well-developed minds, it is debatable whether we have well-developed hearts. A sobering thought but, in the final analysis, one which confronts us with a choice of the type of Singapore we want our youth to reflect. A Singapore of hubristic swagger and self-centredness, or a Singapore of humanist philosophy, civic-mindedness, and sense of duty to family and flag?

Trends, No. 41, *Business Times*, weekend edition, 29–30 January 1994

Critiquing the arts and popular culture

chapter 17

What sort of culture should Singapore have?

Philip Jeyaretnam

"What sort of culture should Singapore have?" is a question that has been tossed about in recent months, rather like a *roti paratha*, whirling in the hands of its maker. Disguised in this question are two separate but related concerns.

First, how do we create a unifying culture of national community? And secondly, how do we become a society of rich cultural opportunities?

In answer to these concerns, and apparently running them together, some say a pressure-cooker is needed, a melting pot that will turn all ingredients into a single tasty mush. Others say that, far from having a melting pot, we must prepare three (or sometimes more) separate dishes, each with its own unique flavour.

I find both answers equally unsatisfactory, for they both rest on a misconception, misled, perhaps by the metaphors they employ, into what might be called the "chef in the tall, white hat" fallacy. The fallacy lies in the belief that we can and ought to shape and direct our culture in the way that a chef prepares a banquet: choosing the type and proportion of ingredients and selecting a particular style of cooking.

I will argue that the growth of a shared and lively culture cannot be planned or centrally directed in this way. Only culture of an active, self-directing sort, the banquet (if one must continue with this misleading metaphor) that prepares itself, is genuinely healthy and genuinely shared; culture that must be officially prompted and centrally directed is passive, as anaemic and lifeless as, yes, the dough which the *roti paratha* maker kneads and pulls, flicks and whirls.

What the chef does wrong?

For those who would advise the chef, the two principal points at issue have been: what ingredients should be used, and what style of cooking should be adopted. In my view, neither of these is a meaningful question.

The question of ingredients is usually taken to refer to a choice between Asian and Western values, between, shall we say, *roti paratha* and the hamburger, or else that judicious mix of East and West, *roti john*.

Some people say we must choose traditional Asian values instead of Western ones. This assertion contains a number of unfounded assumptions, the debunking of which, although not central to my thesis, is none the less illuminating.

First of all, the reason given, that we are Asians, is an argument from what is to what ought to be, identical in form to the proposition that because men are by nature wicked we ought to behave wickedly. Added to this is the sinister twist that an Asian who does not behave as an Asian ought to is somehow "mixed-up", as though societies did not evolve, and as though anyone could seriously model their behaviour on that of, say, two centuries past.

Secondly, a false opposition is being set up between Asian and Western values, when in fact the real contrast is between traditional and modern, between values like deference to status and authority (mirroring a feudal social structure) and values like equality of persons before the law (mirroring the contract-based structure of the market economy).

The shift from feudal society to market economy has, to take one among many changes, altered the distribution of income and economic power within families. No longer does the patriarch control the family's land, its only source of wealth, so that he can demand, and obtain, unquestioning obedience even from his adult children.

The market economy has given children economic independence at an earlier age, so that (leaving aside the natural ties of love and affection) the relationship between parents and adult children must increasingly be built on mutual respect.

Another example of these changes lies in the way we approach traditional Asian art, music or drama. We now bring a modern cast of mind to our traditional art-forms — buying tickets for a performance of Peking Opera, or viewing ceramics in a museum, for example — modern because both the concert hall and the museum are modern concepts. A traditional approach to, say, traditional theatre, would either be participatory, as in street theatre, or else involve the relationship of patron/protector and client/dependent, in the way that rich and powerful Chinese families kept in-house troupes for after-dinner amusement.

In short, we deceive ourselves if we think that "Asian" values are the last and unquestionable word, from which we depart at our peril, not least because their social and economic underpinnings have in many cases disappeared.

This does not mean that we must adopt identical values to those of any other country, even assuming (wrongly) that societies choose their culture like a man his clothes. What it means is that the values of society have to be continuously re-worked with the participation of all its members, reacting to (and perhaps facilitating) economic and social changes.

The second question, that of the appropriate cooking style, again does not seem a meaningful question.

Imagine applying these two different cooking styles to the

development of dance. If one applies pressure-cooker integration, one is apt to achieve a rather bizarre cultural mix: one can imagine a dance form where the movements of the feet are from classical Chinese dance, those of the torso and head from Bharata Natyam, and those of the hands from traditional Malay dance.

If, however, one insists on separate development, then one is likely to achieve an "Instant Asia" parade, a succession of contrasting dances from the different roots of Singapore, none influencing or acquiring resonances from another. These dances would be pale imitations of past manifestations of those vigorous roots, which, in China, Malaysia or India, would continue evolving. None of the dances likely to result from either approach will have much relevance to our concerns in modern Singapore.

Both of these approaches fail because they apply the techniques of social engineering. The idea that people are dough to be shaped in the creation of some cultural end is wholly opposed to the attainment of a truly vigorous culture.

Culture involves engaging our thoughts and feelings, our hearts and minds. Social engineering, by treating people as means, denies that we have the capacity to set our own goals, in short, denies our capacity for thought and feeling. Nor can social engineering produce a genuine sense of national community.

The pressure-cooker approach is likely to fail because the element of coercion will tend to generate resistance: any "official" definition of Singaporean-ness will limit the individual's possibilities for self-fulfilment and probably breed resentment.

The "separate dishes" approach on the other hand will impede the growth of a sense of national community by its insistence that Singaporeans are only true to their real selves if they adhere to their ancestral, pre-Singaporean traditions.

Letting the banquet prepare itself

The best strategy for ensuring a cultural feast, for all Singaporeans as a national community, is to tell the chef to leave the kitchen. Leave it to individuals to make their own choices. This strategy should apply not only to our artists but to all Singaporeans: a vibrant culture presupposes the active participation of all.

This participation will not occur unless Singaporeans are treated as mature adults, entitled to make their own cultural choices. The fundamental institutions underpinning a vigorous culture are, first of all, a commitment to tolerance, established in the institutions of liberal democracy. Pre-eminent among those liberal institutions is freedom of expression, which must be secured to all, whether in the press, in the academic world, on stage or in fiction.

Liberal institutions protect the expression of diverse points of view, heresies as well as established orthodoxy. Liberal institutions provide the social glue which enables the mutually peaceful pursuit of varied goals.

Secondly, there must be a shared language (if not of expression then of translation) for this cultural dialogue, which in Singapore, for better or worse, has principally become some form of more or less "standard" English with a local flavour. A shared language creates a common readership which, in turn, establishes a sense of community. Reading a Singaporean book, addressed to Singaporean readers, I become aware of those other readers, personally unknown to me, yet now part of an imagined community of Singaporeans.

If these fundamental institutions are put in place the stage is set, at the level of "high" culture, for the blossoming of many different artistic visions.

Given the many and varied traditions which have influenced Singapore, we are likely to see attempts to explore and transform those traditions, something of which we begin to see hints in, for example, the plays of Kuo Pao Kun. It is precisely his experimental and modern treatment of ancient traditions that gives his work the potential to be uniquely Singaporean.

This natural re-working of traditional values to meet a modern context (and of modern values to meet a Singaporean context) should be allowed (neither forced nor hindered) to take place at all levels.

It seems easy, yet it will take a fundamental change of attitude. The temptation on the part of government to interfere, to shape and direct, must be resisted. A lively culture cannot be created by decree. It must depend upon the participation of individuals, free to express themselves in their search for the meaning of life.

There is a stark choice: trust Singaporeans to have maturity in freedom or else do not seek or expect a "vibrant culture". Be content instead with culture by committee, overseeing the importation of selected foreign cultural groups or the production of bland local fare. If Singaporeans are treated as children, we will act like children, demanding treats in the shape of big-name touring groups but unable to create a lively cultural dialogue. Without that dialogue, we will not achieve a sense of national community, of having something to say to one another as Singaporeans.

For me, the answer is obvious, the chef should doff his tall, white hat and put his feet up. The kitchen is in place; let the banquet prepare itself.

Trends, No. 1, *Straits Times*, 27 September 1990

chapter **18**

The West, popular culture, and Singapore

Sanjay Krishnan

Shakespeare or Schwarzenegger? In terms of experience, the West of "high cultural" disciplines can be quite remote from the "low" West that impinges daily on the lives of individuals. The latter, however, is rarely thought to merit serious attention. This is especially ironic since TV culture, to name but one aspect of "popular" culture, exerts no small influence over the ways in which individuals today make sense of their lives and their environment. This fact is linked to the increasing control that these cultural forms exercise over the individual subject on what he or she believes it possible to think and do. But more on this later.

A comprehensive list of popular culture would include everything from celebrating religious festivals to eating at hawker centres; popular culture is the culture of the masses, in its widest sense. Mediated through the West, this term finds itself represented by a cluster of powerful manifestations — one major example being the television screen.

Let us start with a brief consideration of how Singapore represents itself to itself through the mass media. Privately produced

TV commercials, for instance, often create scenarios of fantasy and affluence, notably as understood in Western terms.

A commercial for a bank shows a shamelessly greedy English porter flattering a quietly amused character played by Lim Kay Tong. The commercial ostensibly portrays the porter's attempts to identify the latter's country of origin. But at the same time the audience knows, of course, that "Lim Kay Tong" is from Singapore. The commercial succeeds on the basis of this foreknowledge; everyone is winking over the naive porter's shoulder.

The joke also acts as a bond: the viewer is openly encouraged to identify himself with the wealthy Singaporean who has turned the tables on his erstwhile colonial masters. "We" can play by their rules and win — this is what the impeccably attired "Lim Kay Tong" suggests by his refusal to even look the Cockney-accented porter in the face.

How largely do such fantasies of usurpation figure in the social unconscious? Perhaps there are two stories to be told. On the one hand, people go on living in HDB flats, working from day to day, and relating to family and immediate community in ways that are traditionally familiar. The "Singapore" imagined here is an entity shaped in part by its colonial past and by hard work that has paid off in socio-economic terms, united and divided by a variety of ethnic and religious practices; in short, a hybrid that is both more and less a nation.

There is, however, another side to this entity: this is the "Singapore" of rap music and expensive cross-trainers, of fashion boutiques and pseudo-American accents, of handphones and country clubs. Mass media representations, through commercials and film, offer a popular image of the West that is centred on the notion of a particular "lifestyle", enjoining the local consumer to embrace it without necessarily requiring identification or critical reflection.

Shopping, particularly at Christmas, is a good example of this phenomenon; a culture of shopping has evolved in which people are encouraged to spend for no reason other than that it is good to spend. This form of circular reasoning finds parallels in other related areas, one instance being the fashion industry, obsessed as it is with the endless reproduction of novelty and style for their own sake. In this regard, it is commonly argued that consumer culture confines itself to the creation of demand, and desire which can never be satisfied; that it has nothing to do with "culture" in its larger sense. Such a claim could not be further from the truth.

Let us stay with the idea of fashion's endless difference, or its repetition of difference. Repetition is a significant feature of the cultural forms that we have been describing. From the TV sitcom, produced according to a formula of one-joke-every-10-seconds, to the amazing stunts of the Hollywood action movie; from the last "Unbelievable Sale!" to the rhythm of the latest dance track, it is the same difference as the individual is repeatedly shocked into numb pleasure by a set variety of basic stimuli. Unlike, say, traditional ritual, the repetition here does not signify anything beyond itself: all you see is all it means.

In this light, the issue of cultural identity — a matter much discussed of late — and where it is going, becomes one of pressing concern. Wailing self-righteously about the influence of a "decadent" or "individualistic" West is not going to help. As Singapore enters the next century, some of its new challenges need to be seen as the partial consequence of its embrace of the international culture of consumption.

It is possible to see the very concept of "identity" becoming less stable. In itself, this process may or may not be desirable as the local teenager grows up eating samurai burgers, admiring Hulk Hogan, preferring rap to reggae, wearing T-shirts displaying Van Gogh sunflowers, and being permanently plugged into Japanese technology.

The question is whether this lifestyle results in a pleasant limbo of undifferentiated assimilation or in the condition exemplified by the "Lim Kay Tong" character, where cultural essence is defined by hollow mimicry. In either case, it has become increasingly difficult to speak of an inner, inviolable "self". The mass media forms part of a network of global forces that shapes the individual — from the workplace to the home — in more intimate ways than has hitherto been thought possible.

Everything that has been discussed here finds important echoes in a media event in 1991: the Gulf War. The images broadcast over satellite cumulatively told a story which did not require much explanation. Like a simple action movie, there were endless images of Stealth fighters taking off, bird's-eye views of laser-guided missiles finding their targets with incredible accuracy, bridges and buildings collapsing in slow motion, and so on. The political and historical issues surrounding the conflict were largely ignored as the war was unambiguously represented by the media as a straight fight between the forces of good and evil.

No wonder, then, that the war was a hugely "popular" event from start to finish.

Media attention is directed constantly at the "latest" events, on going "live". Such emphasis on the immediate, the now, necessarily spells the beginning of the end for historical consciousness (note how this ties in with the instability of cultural identity). The news, as with fashion and other related cultural forms, teaches us to focus solely on the present, even as it subjects itself to constant change.

We are bombarded from one moment to the next by an unceasing flow of images and information that need to be processed. Time is unconsciously experienced as a totality of unrelated knowledge-filled moments. It is tempting to see a correlation between this condition and the evident lack of historical awareness or interest among Singaporean students, trained as they are within an educational system that emphasizes the ability to rapidly assimilate and process vast amounts of information.

In a world where computer and TV screens lock us into a gigantic network of global communications, in an international situation controlled by the distribution and consumption of information, it goes without saying that the term "culture" needs to be understood and negotiated differently. Quite simply, we need to learn how to imagine the world in a new way.

Trends, No. 15, *Sunday Times,* 24 November 1991

chapter 19

The arts and the market

Stella Kon

As a playwright, what I want is for more and more Singaporeans to see more plays, so that they will create demand for theatre tickets, so more producers will pay me more commissions. That's my simple-minded version of arts promotion. All I need is a marketing strategy, publicity, and a favourable mention by the press.

When talking "arts promotion" what arts are we talking about? What is "promotion"? And (please excuse the silly question) why do we want to promote the arts anyway?

"Arts" could include the fine arts, ballet and opera, loved only by hard-core culture vultures; don't talk commercial marketing, one would surely fail. And they could include applied arts, design, fashion — now you can really see the dollar signs lighting up. Somewhere in between is the great world of entertainment, glamour, and glitz.

As an artist, I feel there are three things I want to keep surviving and growing in my field. They are my basic survival needs; and the opportunity to do my own thing my own way; and for there to be someone out there who will listen, hear, and appreciate what I am trying to do.

How would market forces help me? I would quite like them to work for me the way they worked for Michelangelo (the painter, naturally, not the turtle). Pope Julius II sponsored Michelangelo for a total of 10 years' work on the Sistine Chapel, his private chapel. But Michelangelo did it his own way. He stretched the boundaries of his medium and disregarded existing artistic conventions, ignoring Julius' instruction to paint G-strings on his full-frontal nudes. Michelangelo wouldn't compromise his artistic standards for the client's sake, and being recognized top of his profession, he got away with it.

On the other hand, I certainly wouldn't want market forces to treat me like they treated Van Gogh. Big irony, Van Gogh couldn't sell his work, lived poor, and shot himself in despair. Now when it's too late for him, his paintings fetch multi-digit prices.

Anyway, if we're talking market forces, different arts come to market in different ways. Performance arts — ballet, music, theatre — go by ticket sales. Visual and plastic arts produce (hopefully) sellable objects — paintings, tapestries, pots. Then there are media arts — films, videos, computer graphics. All these are more or less marketable.

There are dying folk arts like handicrafts, oral literature, traditional dances, and theatre forms. Apart from curio shops and museums, no one is interested in paying money for them; well that's why they are dying. Reviving them would need large transfusions of institutional money.

Then there is literature — fiction and poetry — subject to the economics of publishing. The conventional wisdom of the Singapore book trade says that the only commercial success is in school textbooks. (I've written a novel, but you'll probably never hear about it unless I can get ten thousand schoolchildren to read it in class).

And I believe most books of poetry end up as useful bookshelf-supports, in the homes of the poet and his friends. But I did see some poetry in a place where it presumably earned the poet some money — as a poster in the London Underground. The transport authority runs this series of poetry-for-the-commuter as a public service — Singapore Mass Rapid Transit please note.

To me, promoting the arts in Singapore means improving the standard of art to where our output gains international recognition. It means getting more people to patronize art as consumers. I also want to see more Singaporeans become creative producers of art — not only as dedicated professionals, but also at an amateur, recreational level.

Can market forces raise artistic standards? It seems not, if you look at some box-office successes which are artistic junk. On the other hand, "commercialism" doesn't have to be a dirty word. I have friends who have been making their artistic living in the Singapore market-place for years. Like Michelangelo, they know about getting market forces to help you to do what you want to do. They know the discipline of maintaining artistic integrity against the threat of bankruptcy, on one hand, and the temptation of easy commercial crowd-pleasing, on the other.

Working to a client's commission need not be artistically stultifying; it can be challenging and stimulating to find the way to do what the client wants you to do, in the artistic way you want to do it.

Artists can also get support from "sponsors". Sponsorship still comes with some strings attached. Trailing behind government sponsorship are these great tangles of red tape — name your own examples. But the Government has sponsorship monopoly of the infrastructure — rehearsal halls, school halls, etc. Who can afford to offend it? The trouble is that the Singapore artistic market is too circumscribed. Not enough free choices exist among artists, among sponsors, among consumers.

Chairman Mao proposed to "Let a hundred flowers bloom, let a thousand schools of thought contend". No matter that he reneged on his promise of liberalism, and his Cultural Revolution turned absolutely revolting, he correctly noted that art thrives on diversity, and the freedom to experiment. The danger of market pressure is that it discourages artists from being innovative and trying risky experiments. Wider markets would decrease the risk.

Poor Van Gogh lost out because a narrow, parochial European art market didn't appreciate him. (Van Gogh was inspired by Japanese prints. If only his canvases could have been shown in Tokyo a century ago. Would the Japanese of those times have grabbed his stuff, the way they are doing today?)

In Britain, opening up television to a host of private-sector producers seems to have raised standards. The independents have challenged the BBC out of the deadly conservatism of a monolithic statutory body. But "the Beeb", as a non-commercial body, has been able to set a standard for the independents to emulate that is a lot higher than the standard of American commercial television.

My lesson for Singapore is not that SBC should set our artistic standards, but that there is an important role for both government sponsorship, and for a private sector which is much bigger, more competitive than at present.

If Van Gogh were alive today, and doing his revolutionary kind of painting, probably someone — somewhere — would recognize his genius. But if he were a Singaporean, he'd probably have to go abroad to find sponsorship.

Promoting art also means encouraging people to be more interested in the arts. In Singapore we tend to think this should be done in school, that it is the job of the Ministry of Education.

There's plenty of international expertise available on the best way to introduce art into education. However, the Ministry's hands are tied to some extent because it cannot make the really radical changes in school structure that would be needed, and they can't change the nature of Singaporeans.

The kids get arts subjects added to the existing curriculum, but unfortunately no extra hours added to the existing twenty-four in a day to allow for rehearsals and practice. And when "arts" become formal classroom subjects, I fear Singaporeans will kick in the same attitudes of competition, élitism, and fear-of-failure. So arts in the curriculum still needs more conviction and more commitment from educators and parents; the kids themselves are usually keen enough, and frustrated by the various roadblocks that still exist.

Anyway, it's so Singaporean to relegate art education to the schools, implying that grown up people will put aside such "childish" things.

To arrive at a population of cultured, art-loving Singaporeans, the government could harness those famed market forces: cash incentives and tax rebates. We would then have yuppies outbidding each other for local paintings, executives rushing from work to seminars on appreciation of modern sculpture, factory workers getting time off for company-organized sessions of finger-painting and flower-arrangement.

But why do we want all this to happen? Why do we want Singaporeans to be artistic? Or is "art for art's sake" reason enough? There are good pragmatic reasons for teaching the arts to the young, similar to the reasons for encouraging sport. If you have ever taken part in a school play or concert, chances are it would have been one of the most memorable events of your school life. It taught you teamwork and co-operation. It was an experience of working for some great goal (i.e. artistic excellence) which wasn't defined by grades and examination. You were part of something much bigger than yourself.

A young friend of mine gained much more self-confidence and joy in life when she discovered her own unexpected creative talent. She found she could do much more than she thought she could do — it was the homely art of decorating cakes with icing — and it lit up her daily life, as everything she looked at became a possible subject for her new gift.

People who participate creatively in art, making their own art decisions, setting their own goals and standards for their wood-carving or pottery or singing, are more likely to be participators in government, too, instead of just being consumers. In their art they have experienced change and innovation as being promising and exciting, not threatening.

They become more open-minded. In art there isn't one right answer, but there are many possibilities. There isn't one rigid standard to measure everything by; there are many factors to be weighed up, using all the perceptions that God gave us.

Looking at paintings and sculpture, and listening to music increase our emotional sensitivity. Novels and plays make us more aware of other people's outlooks, feelings, and aspirations.

Both the government and private sector can play a part in transforming us into a kinder, gentler nation. One day we may bury the image of the "Ugly Singaporean". In his place we would have the "artistic Singaporean", less materialistic, less self-centred, sensitive to other people's needs. And yet still Singaporean enough to know how to harness market forces to achieve artistic ends.

Trends, No. 12, *Sunday Times*, 25 August 1991

chapter 20

New reach for Singapore's English-language theatre

Robert Yeo

When Singaporean dramatists began to write plays in significant and sustained numbers, the theatre found its identity as a national theatre. This occurred from 1984 onwards in the English-language theatre and the growth since then has been nothing short of phenomenal. That it involves the English language does not make it any less national as these plays reflect and interpret the multi-racial nature of Singapore society more than plays in the other languages.

The progress of this theatre in the mid-1980s will be seen, I am certain, as one of the more momentous and dramatic success stories in the general development of the arts since 1965.

The reasons for its success is reasonably well-known in theatre circles but the general public has very likely only a sketchy idea of how it came about. From 1965 onwards, it was very rare for a Singaporean play to be staged; standard plays from the Anglo-American or European repertoire were regularly staged undisturbed by the occasional play from Third World countries.

From the point of view of developing a national and indeed nationalist tradition, there were several things wrong with this state of affairs. First, it perpetuated the notion that it was all right for multi-racial Singaporeans to pretend that they were British or American or European. Was it not, after all, the logical thing to do — to stage plays we studied? Their obvious Singapore English accents could not cope with the artistic necessity of speaking accurately in, for instance, a J.B. Priestley play, and this showed the moment they spoke. Secondly, they did not look British. Thirdly, the plays were not about us at all. Singapore was going through a period of accelerated transformation which generated hundreds of ideas for plays; the foreign play could not, of course, reflect the change, let alone interpret it.

Theatre had to move to the next phase, the one that produces plays for us, about us and by us. Many plays of the pre-1984 phase purported to cater for Singapore audiences who went because the majority among them thought they would support art regardless of origin. Soon, it became clear to them that to see a Singaporean play was to nourish the beginnings of a nationalist tradition.

Compared to the situation prior to 1984 when a rare play was written and the playwright had to hesitantly locate a director who would then scout for a group if he did not have one, the playwright today is very lucky to have a host of young, talented directors and theatre managers risking new plays.

We now have a theatre-friendly infrastructure: government promotion, funding and facility-provision and, from the public sector, a measure of funding. The theatre community has responded: groups have professionalized, beginning in 1984, paving the way for more regular and better performances. New, amateur groups mushroomed, which encouraged more writing, workshopping and performance. Young and talented people, adept at directing, managing, attracting funds and publicizing their activities, popped up with new and interesting programmes that attracted young audiences at frequently sell-out performances.

The theatre, however, is not completely absorbed with things local. International contacts were made, some through the Arts Festival (which brought to Singapore a playwright of the stature of David Henry Hwang), enabling experts from Taiwan, England, the United States, China and Indonesia, among others, to run workshops and seminars, so as to pass on their skills to local participants. Singaporeans went abroad on Fulbright Hays or British Council sponsored programmes to learn about aspects of the theatre.

The future

What should be the future direction of Singapore theatre? First, the writing and performance of our own plays must go on. I am confident that it will go on because the pillars of the theatre community, the dramatists, the groups, the government, the public sector, and audience, have discovered what it means for an art form to find its identity. The ideological battle has been won, the will is strong and the infrastructure present.

Secondly, theatre documentation is necessary to indicate what has gone on since 1984, a period which has seen exponential growth. Previews, interviews, reviews, and publication of plays present only a partial picture; but a full, scholarly picture of who has written what, how many have been staged, by which groups, what sort of plays, what trends, etc. has yet to be written. We need a well-researched account of the English-language theatre since 1984 (and before, taking into account the brief flowering in the early sixties with the plays of Lim Chor Pee and Goh Poh Seng) to show the extent of progress and future directions. A theatre journal to publish the new plays will be an essential part of this enterprise.

Thirdly, theatre criticism must develop to keep up with the dynamic change. The present situation is unsatisfactory. Newspaper and television reporters fresh from universities, with degrees in English or drama, are put on the theatre beat (from which they will move on, to other beats like travel or food). Their reviews, with exceptions, are characterized by the following: faulty knowledge of facts about the play or about what has relevantly been done in the last five years; description of the play they would rather see than what was actually seen; hasty judgment, often in the form of dubious generalizations; and either vague criteria about what makes a good play or assumptions which fail to take into account some of the constraints of the theatre at the moment.

What is sorely needed is not reportage on plays but theatre criticism that establishes clear, comparative criteria about what makes for a successful play, a firm knowledge of the latest thinking about theatre theories and their applications to Singapore, understanding of the processes of play-making from conception to production and a sympathetic commitment to the kind(s) of theatre which could develop in Singapore.

Everyone recognizes that the English-language theatre is the most developed; everyone, that is, except the Singapore Broadcasting Corporation (SBC). Some years ago, SBC reluctantly agreed to record and telecast short plays; the collaboration left unpleasant memories in the minds of the people involved. Meantime, there are rumours that SBC is about to take English-language drama seriously, rumours which have been around for about half a dozen years. Are we to wait that long before we can expect to view English-language television plays? Are we expected to continue to put up with SBC's excruciating dubbed-in-English versions of Mandarin serials while waiting for the genuine article?

Finally, the theatre could receive an additional boost if awards are given for good performance. Literature has its local and regional awards but, apart from the Shell Short Plays awards, theatre has none. Years ago, awards were given out in various categories for excellence in the Drama Festivals; many who participated remember the competitive camaraderie it generated among contending groups. Naturally, the decisions were controversial and Shell, as the sponsor, was understandably unhappy and the awards were withdrawn. It robbed subsequent drama festivals of friendly rivalry and the opportunity was lost for the heightened comparison of plays which would have further raised standards and brought the theatre community (which is numerous in the proliferation of big and small, professional and amateur groups) together. Competition should be renewed, and the technical details worked out; there could be one festival or productions (and categories of quality) that compete and are judged throughout the year. The National Arts Council is a national body and it could organize this or initiate it.

If this is done, in addition to the other reasons I have advanced for the development of theatre, especially the English-language theatre, there is no reason why it cannot develop further into a regional and international force.

Trends, No. 18, *Sunday Times*, 23 February 1992

chapter 21

Being obsessed with things sexual in the arts

Geraldine Heng and Janadas Devan

If you were one of the Singaporeans who watched Tan Tarn How's *The Lady of Soul and Her Ultimate "S" Machine* in January 1993, what dominant memory, what striking, powerful image of the play did you carry away with you as you left the theatre? Was it the play's "liberal" message ("down with censorship; let a million flowers bloom") that ran uppermost in your mind? Or were you struck instead by that pliantly fleshy, naked, larger-than-life sex doll who provided pneumatic ecstasy to all the men on stage with such lubricious abandon?

It was the doll, of course, hands down. The moment she made her visually sensational entrance, all gigantic buttocks and breasts, bouncing and swaying, compliantly servicing one man after another, the political message was helplessly eclipsed. Limping away from our attention, it yielded the stage to the substantially juicier and fleshier competition.

Why should a play that offers itself as a political satire dealing with a serious subject — censorship — subvert itself visually like this? And why make a worthwhile point about freedom of expression with an adolescent's sex joke, borrowed from a B-grade movie for teenage boys? Why accompany a plea for greater social, political, and cultural freedoms with a lurid joke that acts out the trivialization of those precious freedoms.

Indeed, Tan's play may stand as an example of a curious trend in Singapore today; the fact that the relaxation of censorship controls in the arts often seems to produce, not serious forms of social and political exploration, critique, and questioning — as so often happens in countries where censorship laws are suddenly liberalized — but an obsessed fascination with sexual expression instead.

Apart from a few bold experiments — plays that treat difficult issues like homosexuality or transvestism, for instance — this fascination with sexual matters often takes the form of mere garden-variety luridity. What is presented is closer, in its sexual mores and obsessions, to Penthouse or Hustler magazine, than to anything you might recognize as radical, bold, or politically progressive. Where artists elsewhere might say that the treatment of sexuality can be politics by a different name — since the sexual is the political — producers of cultural texts in Singapore would seem to say, in reverse, that the political is only the sexual, is only sex-as-usual.

Take the curious example of another cultural text, a novel that self-consciously advertises itself as political in subject and treatment: Gopal Baratham's A *Candle or the Sun*, now taught in a compulsory freshman literature course at university level in Singapore. This novel generated a controversy of sorts in 1992 when it failed to win the top prize in the National Book Development Council's bi-annual awards. An imputation was even advanced at one point that its non-selection suggested a failure of political nerve on the part of the judges.

Those who have actually read this novel, including students, often observe, however, that the novel is as memorable for its remarkable sexual fascinations as for its political allegory. Indeed, the political allegory is represented only by a pallid group of characterless young people whose activity seems vaguely confined to a kind of mild civic liberalism (distributing pamphlets calling for more freedom of expression) and the singing of songs with a religious flavour. By contrast, the novel's sexual offerings involve a panorama of vivid, colourful characters, who offer everything from close-ups of frequent sexual couplings, to foul-mouthed language, to such choice titillations as voyeurism and telephone sex.

The dominant memory from this cultural text is of two Indian characters — a grossly fleshy secretary-as-whore, who reeks simultaneously of sexual victimage and invitation, and her foul-mouthed male boss, who possesses a pornographic imagination of astonishing virulence. Once again, the attention of a cultural text that would present itself as social and political critique is split and undermined by its own obsession with sexual display. The most striking, powerful images that imprint themselves on our attention come, not from political critique, but from the salacious conjunction of sexual and racial stereotypes: the pungent celebration of sex-and-race-as-usual.

Why are political intentions thus repeatedly diverted or undone? Why is the depiction of sexuality so often lurid? What, in the character of cultural development in Singapore, produces this exasperating deflection of the serious into the trivial? We have no definite answers to these questions, but will canvass here a few possibilities that may point to tentative conclusions.

Firstly, the insistent attention to sex, on the part of cultural producers, may well be a form of political self-censorship, an indication of either the unwillingness or inability (or both) of writers to advance a serious critique of their society. In an atmosphere where the limits of the permissible are still unclear, the sexual might well seem a safer bet than anything overtly political. This may appear a paradoxical assertion — for isn't the sexual almost always what patriarchal authority wishes most to repress? — but it would seem less paradoxical if we consider the nature of the sexuality portrayed. For what is portrayed, far from instigating a critique of values and ideas, merely leaves everything as it has always been, sexually and otherwise.

Take, for instance, *The Lady of Soul*. The pneumatic contraption offered as the means for Singaporean males to lubricate their "souls", is (surprise!) a woman but, conveniently, not a real woman, only a doll, a mere "Machine". The Mama-san who invents this perfectly pliant version of herself to service, without complaint, male fantasy, in effect issues an invitation to each and every man to commit an imaginary rape. The reality of rape, however, is cunningly concealed. After all, what is "raped" repeatedly on stage is only a large rubber ducky shaped like a woman, not a woman at all, especially not a woman who can say "No". With blissful irony, this would-be political play never seems conscious that it is precisely the image of women as, essentially, ultimate "S" machines who cannot, or should not, speak, that authorizes real rapes in the world.

Nothing, thus, in society really changed when the curtain fell and the delightful commotion on the stage ceased. A patriarch who saw the play need only demur that his own daughter, though admittedly an "S" machine herself, should be reserved for one man only; but as for womenkind in general, oh, well ...! "Lie back doll, with your legs apart, and let me" — and at this point, the patriarch might well beat his breast — "get some soul". This might be a daring thing to say or do in this assertively conservative society, but it ain't political by any stretch of the imagination. It is perhaps necessary to add too that it does not advance a particularly progressive political notion either. Contrary to popular prejudice, issuing invitations to imaginary rapes is not exactly on the agenda of Western-educated liberal intellectuals.

It is precisely the seductive equation between sex and rebellion, however, that sustains the hint of the political in these cultural productions. Like naughty schoolboys who get a thrill from sneaking a peep up the skirts of schoolgirls, these productions derive their thrills from breaking the sexual taboos of a conservative society.

Since breaking taboos of any kind, in any manner whatsoever, suggests rebellion, a certain political glamour consequently descends on the challengers of taboos. The equation is as follows: sex = rebellion = the political. The simplicity of this formula may well explain why lurid sexuality is the subject of choice among writers who aspire to a certain political relevance. There is no easier way to be political: pimply 14-year-olds know the trick.

But irresistible as the equation may be — and under certain circumstances, it can indeed function as a tool of social critique — the equation of sex with politics in these cultural productions serves merely as an alibi for the absence of the political. When what is portrayed is the luridity of sex-as-usual, what we get is not the sexual as the political but the sexual in place of the political. The prevailing dispensation in Singapore may well afford few other opportunities to address the political, but we court disaster if our cultural productions are only able to rehearse, like a broken record, a dreary round of adolescent jokes and juvenile protests.

It must be emphasized though that the fault for this depressing possibility is not only the artist's, but also the government's and the public's. For a few years now, almost all discussion about censorship has centred around sexuality. Debate about film classifications, for example, has focused on the allowable limits of sexually explicit scenes, as if censorship affects society only when it prevents art from depicting the coupling of men and women.

Our studied avoidance of almost every other implication of censorship has had the predictable effect of channelling — and thereby narrowing — cultural attention in a single direction: sexuality. The challenge we have inadvertently posed our writers is: try and see how far you can get with rubber duckies, even when what really concerns you is free speech, detention without trial, or the price of beans. In the process, not only has the political and social significance of art been confined, but sexuality too is debased.

All this is a pity, for the exaggerated attention to sexual display diverts genuine talents in the cultural arena, and puts them to ridiculous uses. Gopal Baratham's gifts as a narrator of arresting stories are deflected and trivialized by the indulgent sexual excursion.

Tan Tarn How's enactment of effective political satire in the first half of his play is dissipated in the ensuing sexual farce. More importantly, the attention of the public is also diverted. Even superbly assured artists like Kuo Pao Kun and Arthur Yap will find it difficult to compete with "S" machines and telephonic sex.

In art as in economics, bad money drives out good. The prevailing cultural situation in Singapore threatens to trivialize the variety of genuine talents we do indeed possess. The only way not to waste these talents, we submit, is to extend the permissible boundaries of discourse in Singapore, politically and socially.

Trends, No. 31, *Business Times*, weekend edition, 27–28 March 1993

chapter 22

Self-congratulation: hallmark of the Singapore arts scene

Derek da Cunha

Some time ago, an art critic, Radhika Srinivasan, wrote in the *Straits Times* about how she was once approached by a "self-proclaimed artist", who asked her: "Can you write about me in the press?" When she tried to clarify: "You want me to write about you or your art", the said artist argued, "rather emphatically, that it was one and the same".

Srinivasan then went on to lament: "Modern individualism with elaborate publicity brochures printed at one's own cost, interviews arranged through 'contacts', and larger-than-life posters to promote one's image as an artist, are not only a vulgar sale of the self but also far removed from the search for the spirit within".

Of course, if you cannot persuade an art critic or a journalist friend to write about you and your work, you can always do the job yourself. Sounds tawdry? Well, the fact of the matter is that such a practice is not unknown in Singapore. Just a few months ago a self-styled Singaporean "playwright", who is also a journalist, wrote a favourable review of her play in her own magazine. Perhaps there is truth in what they say about "journalist ethics" — it's an oxymoron.

This brings one to the issue of aspects of incestuousness within the arts and entertainment communities in Singapore, more so than possibly anywhere else given the smallness of the place. The lines of entanglement that bring together the journalistic and artistic professions suggests a level of conflict of interest that is disturbing. And all of this is done in a bid for public adulation.

The true artist would not rely on public adulation, howsoever well-conceived, to build on his beliefs about his talents. Rather, he or she would challenge his or her own beliefs by tearing down the whole structure around which those beliefs had been built. He or she would then start again from scratch with a fresh perspective. Such an approach is the very essence of a constant "search for the spirit within". It is precisely this sort of artistic spirit that distinguishes the great artist from the mediocre.

The trouble is that there is too much of a glorification of mediocre art in Singapore. This is not least because there are few other places in the world where if you write a single, undistinguished, work of fiction, you are presumptuous enough to immediately style yourself a "novelist", and the press will promptly give credence to that view. You write one play and apparently you are a "playwright". You write two plays, remarkable only for their intellectual vacuity, and chances are you will feature on the front cover of some popular magazine or other, indicating to readers the arrival of a new role model.

There are growing numbers of Singaporeans who want to be instant artists, whether as playwrights, novelists, dramatists, classical musicians, painters or whatever. Why? Largely because artistic careers in Singapore are increasingly seen as a valuable social cachet — an easy route to local (one stresses local) fame. In other words, there are some who are getting into a right and honourable profession for possibly the wrong reasons. As a well-known Japanese expatriate industrialist once remarked to *Business Times* Associate Editor Margaret Thomas, "Singaporeans are clever, but the bad thing is that they don't have much patience. They learn things a little bit, and already they think they are experts. Very shallow thinking, because they've never had difficulties before". Many in the arts community manifest this undesirable trait.

Normally, those without a privileged background, with no social connections to speak of, and who desert orthodox career paths in favour of fashioning their own destinies in the arts, would exude a certain single-minded determination and flair. But no. With rare exceptions, the Singaporean species tends to be conformist, imitative, run-of-the-mill, waiting for the authorities to "nurture" their supposed latent talent, doubtless with generous hand-outs.

This image is only too well exemplified by the themes many Singaporean novelists tend to serve up the reading public — deviant sex, American-style slap-stick humour, and the inevitable descent into the supernatural. With all that, one would be forgiven for thinking that these writers have, as Evelyn Waugh might put it, been supernaturally guided to bore the reader. This is not to say that their writing style is uniformly bad. Indeed not, for there are many who seem quite capable of constructing a grammatical sentence. And, in time, they might even surpass themselves by treating us to the prospect of an elegant sentence.

The crux of the issue, however, is that in art it is not a question of perfection or elegance but rather imagination and originality and, within the Singapore context, an alert sense of the contribution that the recondite can make to the beginning of a truly flourishing artistic tradition, which really matters. No one is suggesting that this is easy to achieve, and its numerous and varied lines of development constitute another essay for another occasion.

But, in the meantime, one cannot help but observe that some of the best Singapore-born artists, like internationally-acclaimed concert pianists Seow Yit Kin and Melvyn Tan, and the widely-published Commonwealth Literature specialist Shirley Chew, would rather spend their time in the West, where they are constantly challenged to reach new heights of artistic creativity, than remain in Singapore.

The home-front though is not entirely bereft of artistic excellence, as witness the strength in the work of playwright and artistic director Kuo Pao Kun, novelist Gopal Baratham, and water-colourist Ong Kim Seng. But it will take more than these few to shake off what one outside observer last year referred to as Singapore's "reputation of being a cultural and artistic wasteland". The *cognoscenti* in both Asia and the West would concur.

And it is this which has become a symbol of an admission the local arts community dare not bring itself to make — that despite first-rate facilities and generous levels of public and private sponsorship, most of our so-called "artists" are just not quite up to it, no matter what their self-congratulation might tend to suggest. Perhaps it is time to put aside the self-congratulation and the misplaced egalitarian tendency of bracketing the excellent few with the mediocre many, if the qualitative phase of artistic development in Singapore is truly to take off.

Trends, No. 37, *Business Times*, weekend edition, 25–26 September 1993

Urbanism and the search for space

chapter 23

Understanding a society's needs for space

G.L. Ooi

The space we live, work, shop and relax in, is being increasingly allocated, planned and designed for us. This arrangement works upon the good faith that those who create and design spaces for us, that is, the architects, planners and such policy-makers, fully understand Singaporeans' needs for space. Such an understanding would be reflected in the built-form we see around us and the degree of comfort or otherwise which we derive from using the space thus created for us. It is, therefore, important that the relevance of our understanding a society's needs for space should be reviewed from time to time.

The World Habitat Awards recognition of the Tampines New Town in Singapore as an excellent example of how to organize, administer and construct high quality dwellings in socially cohesive communities suggests that the need for space is far more than a physical need. Researchers who have emphasized the cultural and, generally, the social significance of space have some reason to feel vindicated.

After all, the new town was being recognized for its winning match of society's needs to spatial design. According to the brief account provided on the award-winning new town, "All residents live in their own self-contained flat, 75 per cent being owner-occupiers. Emphasis today is upon choice and upgrading of flats and on improving existing services and facilities". Other qualities which had helped the New Town win were the emphasis given to architectural variety and character, the degree of security because of the virtual absence of crime and the accommodation of people from varying income and racial backgrounds.

The award won by Tampines New Town was, therefore, more than a recognition of the Housing and Development Board's success with public-housing design and spatial planning in its estates and new towns. This award was also given for the successful translation of society's needs for space into built-form. Judging from the award-winning new town and other efforts which have won similar recognition, there is much to look forward to in a relationship between society and space that is being forged in practice and not merely in design or social theories.

Architects and other designers have, in the past, successfully shown off the glory of rulers, religions and cultures. In more contemporary times, they have designed our cities to showcase the power of governments, courts of justice or the clout of big business. Their challenge for the future could lie in the creation of space which the masses can enjoy and develop a sense of ownership over. In Singapore, the HDB's architects have spoken of the design effort in public housing estates and new towns as providing the stage for life's drama and its players. This assumes an understanding of life and its players in order to create a stage design that best serves both.

To arrive at an understanding of society's needs for space, there has to be a bridging of the gap which purportedly exists between the professions which create space and the society they serve because there have been differences in the "language" used by these designers of space and social scientists. Consequently, as one social scientist has loftily observed, social discourse has been conducted at a level that generally has kept it well above the heads of architects and planners. Conversely, the architects and planners, not having been participants in this social discourse, could be expected to have dismissed its consequences to design and the space being created. There have also been more pressing concerns like the considerations of people bankrolling developments.

The difficulty in finding the basis for a common discourse notwithstanding, the architects and planners who have worked on our award-winning new town have to be recognized for having contributed towards a bridging of the gap. This contribution illustrates that there is much to be gained in recognizing that the planning and design of space is more than a physical process. It is very much a social process, and the need for space is both a physical as well as a social need.

Since space is both a physical and a social need, the task of understanding and providing for the need can be complicated. Still, basic needs for living space would be relatively easy to meet compared with the demand on spatial qualities that could develop once a society has gone beyond the basics. Meeting basic needs in living space in the past might have meant providing a roof over people's heads, markets for fresh food and provision shops for groceries. Such needs can be expected to change over time and the changes will, in turn, affect the demand on the quality of spatial planning and provision.

A bid to improve the provision of traditional wet markets for fresh food in Singapore was one such response to society's changing needs for space and its quality. The challenge was, however, in transferring the qualities of the traditional wet markets to new built-forms which would make these an improvement over the traditional markets. A clamouring for the return to traditional "wet" markets gives some indication of the difficulties involved. People liked the new markets but preferred the variety of market stalls, spaciousness, ease of choosing among vendors while comparing prices and freshness, the choices and the whole business of selection and bargaining which had been customarily found in the traditional wet markets.

In contrast, while some film-goers in Singapore might have lamented the passing of the large and grand cinemas of old like the Lido, the multiplex with its cluster of little cinemas offering patrons a choice of several different movies at any one time appears to be contributing to the new interest in cinema-viewing. Some might be inclined to think that the multiplex's contribution pales beside that of the on-off-on again liberalization of film censorship. Other multiplexes are being planned.

There are changes in the offing which should further test the understanding of society's needs for space in Singapore. One of the aims of upgrading public housing is to narrow the gap between public and private condominium housing. In the effort to give public housing residents what they have always needed to make them feel more like private condominium residents, the social and other qualities defining private condominium housing should be considered rather than merely an attempt at replication of the built-form. Likewise in the wish to give the new town of Woodlands Orchard Road-style shops, one looks forward to the serious consideration of the variety, excitement, choice and options that appear to be drawing shoppers to Orchard Road more than a transplantation of the replicas of its shops.

Life, as someone once gloomily contemplated, can be nothing but a passage through boxes: being born in a box, growing up and living in a box and exiting finally, also in a box. It is to be hoped that such a prospect of life can be avoided if society's needs for space are better understood especially by those responsible for allocating, planning and designing it for us.

Trends, No. 30, *Business Times*, weekend edition, 27–28 February 1993

chapter **24**

Key urban challenges amidst rapid change

P.G. Raman

The Urban Redevelopment Authority (URA) recently unveiled the Concept Plan showing how Singapore is going to develop land, transport, housing, industry, leisure and cultural facilities over the next 25 years. The key features of the plan will have low and medium-rise housing complementing the existing and proposed stock of high-rise housing. Efforts to reduce congestion in the Central Business District (CBD) will take the form of four regional centres, a new business district at Marina Bay and two high-technology corridors consisting of 18 business parks. As for transportation, existing expressways and mass rapid transit (MRT) lines will be extended and new ones, including a light rail, will be added. Some 15 new golf courses and several new marinas will be created. About 3,000 hectares of natural landscape, which include some water bodies, will be preserved; so too will the architectural heritage of Singapore.

Urban design could, of course, be discussed as a merely technical and aesthetic matter, but analysing it as a process highly affected by social, cultural and political factors would lead to a better understanding. In this connection, it ought to be said that the crucial urban tasks facing Singapore are not made explicit in the Concept Plan. Our achievements in economic growth, housing and transportation are certainly there for everyone to see. Nevertheless, we have not demonstrated that a high standard of environment can be created side by side with economic growth.

Singapore has lost its essential character as a historic city because we have shaped it on economic rationale alone. New towns simply appear tacked on to devastated central parts. They are asocial and amorphous and follow the dated stereotypical notion of neighbourhood planning. We have not used much of the natural landscape that is possible in our climate as an integral part of the new towns, and where the new towns are in urban settings we have not made them sufficiently vibrant and colourful.

Public housing continues to be second-rate places of residence as opposed to living examples of urban planning at its best. We have not supplemented the car-restraint policies in the central business district with more thoughtful public transport provisions. Finally, we have not protected the historic cores of Chinatown and Little India from encroaching commercialism (the proposal for a Little India theme park is an example), and "gentrification".

To what extent does the Concept Plan address these issues?

Land-use and transportation

A city's transport system is dictated by its land-use policy. Whether we travel miles to work, or cycle or walk, is determined by the pattern of physical development. A city's transport system functions better if things are close to home: the compact layout of cities like Toronto shows that it promotes fewer and shorter journeys and a higher use of public transport. Apart from mentioning the extension and creation of new MRT lines and expressways, the Concept Plan says nothing at all about integrated transportation. Car-dependence seems likely to continue.

The most transport-efficient land-use pattern is indisputably the one which combines a dense, well-mixed downtown with several outlying compact centres of activity — all linked by an extensive public transport system. In this way people can walk, cycle, take short bus trips within a given area and reach others by rapid rail or bus. To that extent, the creation of regional centres is a reasonable concept but there are problems in making it attractive to investors and businesses.

Decentralization

Urban decentralization is certainly a world-wide force in all highly industrialized countries, and the notion of a poly-centric city is laudable. But experience in places like Paris shows that, in spite of positive planning measures, it is not possible to decant sufficient functions to regional centres. Therefore, while decentralization is on everybody's mind in Europe, its enforcement has been rather difficult. The only reasonably successful urban regions of the multi-centred kind are the West Netherlands and the Rhine-Ruhr region in West Germany, both with many historic cities acting as regional nuclei. In both these cases we are talking about regions that are about nine or 10 times the size of Singapore. Therefore, is the notion of five regional centres far too vast a solution to the problems faced by an island-city like Singapore? Our motorcar-centred problems need a much closer study, and only compact growth in the centre, which indeed can occur quickly, can claim back valuable city space from the motorcar. The cities of Curritiba in Brazil and Portland, Oregon, in the United States offer valuable lessons in this respect.

The Concept Plan is certainly optimistic about decanting functions from the CBD to regional centres. Since the new towns in which the regional centres are located have been perceived, in the first place, to be inferior to the old centres, this might prove to be an insurmountable problem. To some extent, Singapore planners recognize these difficulties. For instance, because there is plenty of scope and sites for development in the central area, there is no urgency to develop Marina Bay. However, if the central district is allowed to develop fully, Marina Bay might become less attractive to the developers and hence the decision to start the project there now. But if the new up-market Marina Bay, which is so close to the present CBD, has difficulty in attracting investment, what makes the planners think that other regional centres like Tampines, Woodlands, Jurong East or Seletar would not face these problems?

The housing question

By the year 2030 about 30 per cent of Singaporeans are expected to live in medium- and low-rise housing. This figure is depressingly low for an affluent country and this is partly because we have a legacy of an enormous stock of HDB (Housing and Development Board) high-rise flats, which is continuously being added to. In case there is any misunderstanding, let it be said that no other developing country has solved its housing problem as effectively as Singapore. Nevertheless, there are shortcomings to the HDB-type of housing, and these need to be highlighted.

The HDB layouts follow the stereotypical notion of neighbourhoods of the same pattern with the same catchment sizes of 6,000 families each. Experience elsewhere suggests that, with the improvement of transportation systems, self-contained neighbourhoods are not a viable concept and they need to be replaced with highly interacting, vibrant and mutually competing districts with a degree of specialization in terms of the provisions each offers for culture, recreation and shopping. Considering the volume of housing stock that has been built up since independence, alternative forms of housing with variations in density, layout, mixture of house types and so on have not been explored.

Perhaps our problems may stem from the monopoly which the HDB holds on the construction of public housing — this does not allow local private architects any input into design. The problem with producing an enormous quantity of housing under one agency is that mistakes may be repeated.

Conservation

Restructuring and repairing historic areas ought to be carried out for more profound reasons than just to attract tourists. We ought to see conservation as an integral part of planning and this is also in the long-term interest of a healthy tourism industry. Conservation in most European countries has certainly come to represent the expulsion of ordinary people. It is, of course, all too easy to see conservation in terms of class politics.

Nevertheless, one or two attempts in Europe to deal with these social effects offer some lessons for us. The attempts to preserve the traditional population structure of the Christianborn district of Copenhagen failed because families preferred to live in the suburbs. This might well be the case in Singapore, but do we really know? If this is not the case then the methods adopted in Bologna, whereby the inner city historic area is preserved as a residential zone with a large amount of inexpensive accommodation, is worth our study. The tools used in Bologna are large financial grants, strict controls on change of use, continuous consultation with the residents of each district, and ensuring that grants are made on condition that the original tenants are retained at pre-conservation rents.

Challenges for architects and planners

The foregoing should not be seen as an exercise in finding fault with the Concept Plan. Rather, it has been an attempt at suggesting alternative strategies based on experiences elsewhere. For instance, is it possible to reduce our car dependence through an integrated approach to public and private transportation instead of allowing a tired public transport to chase dormitory towns in the periphery?

Can our workplaces be near our homes? This will help us to go beyond the traditional notion of zoning various functions and, in addition, if we meet most of our cultural and recreational needs near our homes, we are well on the way to achieving urban excellence.

Can we have more innovative forms of public housing? And, can private sector architects make a contribution in developing them? Is it not time that we experimented with some high-density housing in downtown empty sites? Should not decentralization be tried out as a pilot project in one regional centre and its success or failure be monitored in an unbiased way? Can we start some wider discussion on how we can conserve not only the physical fabric but also the traditional activities of historic areas without resorting to dubious ideas like theme parks or, for that matter, turning them into museums of empty buildings?

The Concept Plan is, after all, a broad strategy. It can still be nudged into directions that will benefit Singaporeans from all walks of life, and answers to the questions raised above can influence the tactical decisions in a profound way.

Trends, No. 17, *Sunday Times*, 26 January 1992

chapter 25

Eye on the Concept Plan

John Keung

In October 1991, the revised Concept Plan, a blueprint for Singapore's physical development into the 21st century, was set in front of the Singapore public. The Plan outlines significant improvements in economic and business growth, transport, housing, leisure and the environment. These advances are all linked to the Plan's central theme, i.e. to cater to a population of four million and to provide a better quality of life for all Singaporeans.

But since some time has elapsed — and since there has been considerable discussion and examination of the elements of the Concept Plan — perhaps it is an opportune moment for the Urban Redevelopment Authority to look at some of the feedback.

Firstly, many people tend to look at the Concept Plan proposals in isolation. Some have focused on the leisure proposals, others on transportation, others on business growth. All of these things interlock like the pieces of a jigsaw. The Concept Plan is not a collection of individual proposals; it is a master plan for Singapore's future, which draws all the various parts of our daily lives together to form a big picture. Everything recommended by the Plan harks back to this big picture and to the central theme — to comfortably accommodate a population of four million and provide them with a better quality of life.

We need four million people to help drive and sustain a growing economy. Without that economic growth, few of the benefits proposed in the Concept Plan can be realized. But in a small country like Singapore, we need to plan far ahead to be able to confidently say that we can comfortably accommodate four million people with a better quality of life. That leads us to the benefits: the Plan forms the infrastructure for economic growth and then offers proposals to build on that infrastructure to create an improved quality of life.

Economic/business growth

Some people have questioned the need for the proposed Regional Centres and have hinted that the latter will have a problem attracting investment. The four Regional Centres have only 1.5 million square metres of commercial floor space each. Together, they will make up a total of 6 million square metres by Year X, when Singapore has four million people. That is less than the current Central Area, which has a commercial area of seven million square metres.

By Year X, when Singapore has 4 million people, the Central Area will more than double to 15 million square metres of commercial space. Regional Centres will be big — about 15 times the size of Housing Development Board town centres today — but they will not take over the role of the Central Area. Instead, they are designed to serve up to 800,000 people, to be vibrant mini-cities which bring jobs, shops, social and recreational facilities, restaurants, cinemas and nightlife closer to Singaporean homes.

Official projections show that, with economic growth, alternative sites for commercial growth will be needed with a population reaching four million. This will save the Central Area from being congested by growth. The Regional Centres, which will be in Tampines, Woodlands, Seletar and Jurong East, are ideal locations as they are hubs of our road and rail networks. They will be developed to provide business-men with another choice of location as demand grows. Already, the signs are promising. The Tampines Regional Centre, for instance, al-ready has some "early bird" tenants in Cathay Multiplex, DBS Bank (which is building a $98 million banking and shopping complex) and a CPF branch office.

Other potential tenants include a Telepark (a special telecom-munications infrastructure to serve companies that need sites for their telecommunications, or computer systems and which need access to communications networks immediately) and a Finance Park proposed jointly by the Monetary Authority of Singapore and the Economic Development Board.

Transportation

Many people look at transport in isolation. Most of the feedback we have encountered relates to when the MRT will be coming to "my" area. But there has also been some criticism that the Concept Plan does not say anything about integrated transportation. The Concept Plan is all about integrated transportation. Land uses that attract large numbers of people, such as the commercial centres, will be located where they are well-served by public transportation like the MRT. The integration of land use and transport is a fundamental tenet of the Concept Plan. Coupled with this is the integration between the different transport modes to facilitate transfers between cars, buses, trains and even ferries.

Travelling around Singapore will be easier and more convenient in "the next lap". An island-wide expressway system will be in place, the MRT will be extended, a new light rail system (LRT) will be introduced, special "bikeways" will be built and pedestrian zones created in the city. New expressways and semi-expressways — major roads capable of carrying 7,200 cars per hour, as opposed to existing major roads which can take about 4,500 cars per hour — will be built as part of an island-wide road system. More flyovers and computer-controlled traffic lights will improve traffic flow.

Over 90 new MRT and LRT stations are planned to complement the 42 existing MRT stations. The MRT will be extended first to areas like Woodlands by the Year 2000 and then to new housing areas like Ponggol and Hougang by the Year 2010. It will also be extended from Marina South to Potong Pasir. If the population exceeds four million, Pulau Ubin and Pulau Tekong will also be accessible by MRT.

The LRT will be an overground rail system which carries fewer people than the MRT and links up to the MRT. The LRT will evolve first in the north and north-east before spreading to the west and south of the island. It will link major urban centres like Yishun, Ponggol and Tampines. Connected to the public bus system and the MRT, the LRT will form part of a more highly integrated transport system.

Also planned is an improved ferry system which will serve not only international destinations but also islands earmarked for recreational development (such as the Southern Islands) and industrial growth (such as Pulau Bukom). Five ferry service sectors — one in the Central Area and one more each in the North, West, East and Jurong areas — are planned. The ferry terminals will be connected by MRT, LRT, bus and road — another example of transport integration.

Cyclists and, even pedestrians, figure in the Plan's integrated approach to public and private transportation. The use of bicycles will be encouraged. Bicycle facilities — cycleways and bicycle parks — will be built in new towns so people can cycle to MRT stations or directly to commercial areas. Special, separate "bikeways" will make cycling safer as cyclists will not have to negotiate heavy traffic on the roads.

Housing

Some have asked for more innovative forms of housing. The Concept Plan does address the future wants and needs of Singaporeans in housing by encouraging a greater variety of housing. At present, about 83 per cent of our housing are high-density public apartments and 17 per cent low- and medium-density housing.

The Concept Plan proposes to raise low- and medium-density housing to 30 per cent by Year X. There are now 611,000 high-density homes. The number will almost double to 1.1 million by Year X. At the same time, land will be set aside for more townhouses, maisonettes, semi-detached and terraced houses, bungalows, low- and medium-rise apartment blocks. There are 130,000 such dwelling units today. This will more than treble by Year X. So, although our population will increase by a third, our housing stock will effectively double.

A better quality of life also means having more living space. At present, each Singaporean has an average of about 20 square metres of living space — equivalent to a family of four living in a three-room flat. Over time, that living space will be expanded to 30–35 square metres like that of a family of four living in a five-room flat.

There will also be more variety and choice in housing. Projects like Simpang, Tanjong Rhu and Kampong Bugis will be developed to provide waterfront housing. Simpang, for example, will be a mixture of high-, medium- and low-rise housing in a wide range of styles in a setting that is expected to achieve harmony with the water. In the next 10 years, there will be other new housing areas at Seletar, Sembawang and Ponggol.

There will also be more innovative forms of private housing that will be more within the reach of the public. Land at many HDB areas will be released for sale to the private sector for development as low- and medium-housing. It is envisaged that, with a greater supply of housing with design and facilities similar to those of condominiums, such housing will become more affordable. There will also be smaller landed property lots to make them more affordable to Singaporeans.

Leisure

Leisure is one of the key considerations of the Concept Plan. The leisure plans are far-reaching, such as creating new beaches and islands and offering new sports and recreation facilities, and entertainment and adventure parks. These proposals, while they will be very beneficial and enjoyable to all Singaporeans, also give Singapore a whole new dimension — that of a tropical island playground.

At present, Singapore has a distinctly urban atmosphere. It is possible to come to Singapore and not know that you are on an island. The Concept Plan will change that. The present coastline will be almost doubled from its present 140 kilometres by reclamation to help create a tropical playground with more beaches and more room for resorts, marinas and other waterside leisure activities.

By the year 2010, scenic coastal roads will allow Singaporeans to drive leisurely around the island, with picnic spots and viewing spots established. Resorts and marinas are planned at various sites like Changi Point, Tanjong Rhu, Marina East, Pasir Ris, Simpang and the Southern Islands.

A long island will be reclaimed off the east coast. It will run along the length of the east coast from Marina East to Changi. The island will be a leisure centre by Year X with beaches, more marinas and resorts and some housing development. Other islands, like Pulau Ubin and Pulau Tekong, will keep their natural atmosphere offering camping, hiking, fishing, canoeing, swimming and nature walks.

There will be plenty of other leisure-based improvements. More entertainment parks and adventure parks are planned, with disused quarries as possible sites for adventure parks. Cultural, retail and entertainment centres which house artistic, tourism and cultural events together with shopping arcades are also planned. One such development is planned at Clarke Quay along the Singapore River.

More sports facilities like swimming pools, stadiums, tennis courts, squash courts and golf courses will be built on land set aside for such purposes. By the Year X, the number of public stadia will more than double from 14 to 30. Swimming complexes will increase from 25 to 40, squash and tennis centres from 20 to 35 and water sports centres from 5 to 22. Other facilities — including turf clubs, flying clubs, archery clubs, gun clubs, camping sites and other specialist sports and recreation centres — are also planned.

Plans have also been made for cycle tracks to encircle and criss-cross the island, linking the parks, gardens, natural areas and the coast.

Environment

The Concept Plan consciously tries to build our tropical foliage and "island-ness" into our urban environment. Singapore already has a reputation as a "clean and green" city, and the intention of the Plan is to further shape our environment with greenery and waterways.

The Concept Plan uses the Green and Blue Plan as a kind of environmental base on which leisure and sports and recreation advantages can be built. It proposes to enhance the environment in three main ways — having more parks and gardens, carefully tending the natural foliage and wildlife, and bringing the natural environment closer to urban areas.

At present, there are about 7,500 hectares of natural parks and gardens, sports and recreation grounds and green belt areas in Singapore. There will be about a 30 per cent increase by Year X.

Nature stations — pockets of natural landscape, like hills or wooded areas, river banks and the like — will be conserved near residential areas to help create the image of leaving the busy city far behind. Also earmarked for conservation are some 3,000 hectares of wooded areas, bird sanctuaries, mangrove swamps, water bodies and nature reserves.

Tropical foliage and waterbodies will be woven even more deeply than at present into Singapore's urban structure. The new Downtown area, to be merged with the contours of Marina Bay, is one example. So are parks and greenways developed within new housing areas. Each new town will have town gardens, town parks of about 10 hectares and various neighbourhood parks together with the bigger regional parks like the 30-hectare Bishan Park.

Enhancing our environment includes conserving our architectural and ethnic heritage. The Concept Plan recognizes that our past is an important part of our future, and that our lives are enriched by being able to relate to examples of our culture, origins and ethnic identities. The main activities of conservation are to preserve areas and buildings that are part of Singapore's heritage, despite the commercial application of some conservation projects. This includes areas like Little India, Kampong Glam, Chinatown and the Singapore River.

It can, thus, be seen that the Concept Plan takes into consideration the needs and wants of Singaporeans living in "the next lap" in order to build a Singapore that will not only be home to four million people but a home with an even better quality of life than today's.

Trends, No. 20, *Business Times*, 30 April 1992

chapter 26

A new urbanism communicated by shopping centres

Yao Souchou

In Southeast Asian cities, mass consumption has become an important part of our lifestyle. This is partly due to the rising standard of living as people seek to express their new status aspirations through consumer goods ranging from Nike sports shoes and McDonald's hamburgers to Mercedes Benz cars.

At the same time, telecommunications, labour migration and internationalization of capital also contribute to the globalization of consumer culture that primarily originated in metropolitan centres in Europe and the United States. Some are inclined to look at the process as one of Westernization of local culture and values. Yet it is also true that we have largely appropriated the items of mass consumption and made them a source of our urban identities.

Rightly or wrongly, owning branded designers goods so elaborately advertised and marketed in Asian cities expresses something about our feeling and understanding of the conditions of our existence. In this, we recognize the complex textuality of our needs and desires, and that urban consumers are not mere victims of ruthless commercialism but possess the ability to script our own identities and empowerment.

Architects in Southeast Asia are attempting to express and communicate this new urban reality. The design of shopping centres — the most visible landmark from Jakarta to Bangkok — in particular, aims to articulate the multifarious social experience of shopping, while ensuring their functionality and commercial viability.

The so-called post-modern style has produced at best buildings and urban developments that are eclectic and ironic, flexible and rich, emphasizing context rather than empty abstract form, and at worst a mixture of "non-styles" devoid of personal depth and authentic judgement.

The approach inserts often conflicting design elements on to considerations of formal requirements and efficiency. The result, at least for the supporters, communicates very powerfully the fragmented and multiple nature of our urban lives and values.

In Singapore, this juxtaposition of tradition and innovation, functionality and stylistic freedom is being played out in some very exciting though not faultless architecture. Along the Orchard Road "golden mile", Shaw House and the recently opened Ngee Ann City are retail complexes built on land that is among the most expensive in the world. They both feature columns and outside mantles of polished marble that conceal the building core of steel framework.

The classicism here, however, reminds one of the Graeco-Roman temples rather than anything "Asian". As retail centres, the functional aptness is never allowed to be the sole dictate of the built-form which struggles to express the manifold and diverse nature of use.

Outside Shaw House, one looks down on to a deep open space where sitting benches are built with their backrests curving alternatively to give a series of private sittings within a community of users. Shaw House and Ngee Ann City, which houses the Takashimaya Shopping Centre, the largest retail centre in Southeast Asia, are typical of the new generation of shopping centres.

These urban sites use an architectural language that is playful and functionally diverse in order to communicate and realize the complex social experience of personal consumption. It is a language that recognizes the radical logic that mass consumption is both alienating and empowering, and that retailing has to provide more than just goods and services but a certain lifestyle as well.

These shopping centres may be more appropriately called lifestyle centres. Shaw House contains the anchor tenant Isetan Department Store and the five-theatre Lido 5 Cineplex.

The multi-use principle is even more evident in the Takashimaya Shopping Centre made possible by its immense size of 710,424 square feet. It features, besides the department store, an art gallery, a fitness club, food village, children's playground and a culture centre where you can learn "the finer points of art and craft, language and dance".

A truly multi-functional site like Takashimaya (slogan: "A celebration of life") moves away from the orthodox concept of the shopping centre as a place of economic transaction, but one suggestive of fun, leisure and personal choice.

The design principle also makes sense in the new economics of retail space. Traditionally, shopping centres had depended on the passerby pedestrian traffic as the main catchment of users and potential customers. But with the size and financial capital involved, a new shopping centre like Ngee Ann City is able to create its own catchment of users attracted by the myriad of facilities provided — boutiques, "food village" and World Gourmet Street, supermarket and children's corner. In this "city within a city" people come not only to buy but also to look, stroll and wander.

Takashimaya is part of the current trend which places retailing around crowd-drawing facilities like the cinema, food court and hotels. Further south of Orchard Road, on Stamford Road, is Raffles City designed by the American-Chinese architect I M Pei. Sitting on a 216,000 square feet site, Raffles City consists of a series of buildings interrupted by an open atrium. The shopping mall sits in the mid section flanked by two five star hotels — the Westin Stamford (1,253 rooms and 16 restaurants) and the Westin Plaza (796 rooms and 16 restaurants).

A broad atrium leads directly from the mass rapid transit (MRT) station to the mall. After alighting from the City Hall Station, entry to the malls is interrupted by the open space where people gather their thoughts, meet friends and decide what to do next. It is as if the atrium has been designed to interrupt the otherwise direct flow of traffic from the MRT station to the mall opposite.

The mall itself is sparse with a distinct sense of austerity. The feeling is created by the internal atrium at the centre which, as one looks upwards to the roof, pushes the shops "against the wall" to the sides. As the dominant space of the mall, the internal atrium also breaks the visual connection from shop to shop from one side to another. Leaving a shop on the first level, one sees immediately not the shops opposite but the space underneath where sales, exhibitions and cultural shows are held.

The design approach achieves a sense of spatial democracy where open spaces and the atrium rather than retail shops appear to be the dominant features. By encouraging people to loiter, and make use of the facilities whether they are buying or not, Raffles City seems to express a disavowal of its commercial intent by emphasizing the importance of public spaces.

The retail complex communicates the insight that commercial viability can be achieved by targeting not at a relatively small number of "real" shoppers, but the larger public of uncommitted mall users who can be seduced by the stratagem of advertising fantasy. In this sense, it is typical of the urban site in our rapidly changing cities: a mixture of functionality and amusement, economic sense and commercial allurement.

Trends, No. 36, *Business Times*, weekend edition, 28–29 August 1993

The economy: new directions, old problems

chapter 27

Corporate networking: where to next?

Arun Mahizhnan

Over the past 25 years or so, Singapore has developed many variations of what is known as "corporate networking" in its efforts to sustain economic growth. Some of these have come in the form of the symbiotic relationship among labour, management and the government; the multi-agency network within the government to help local enterprise; manpower development through joint training institutes run by the private sector and the government; a network of financial assistance schemes supported by the public and private sectors; the local industry upgrading programme that hitches local suppliers to multinational corporations for mutual benefit.

Let us now look at four new areas in which corporate networking is likely to make its mark.

Fusion concept

In what the Economic Development Board (EDB) calls the fusion concept, local enterprises are encouraged to form a coalition of strategic partners that will develop, produce and market products that members are not likely to have done individually. The fusion concept brings together individual but complementary capabilities for specific joint projects. This kind of networking is rather new to Singapore and no empirical data is available to make a serious assessment. However, it is an approach that tries to take advantage of the complementarity that already exists within the industry and is, therefore, likely to succeed.

SIF network

The Singapore International Foundation (SIF), established in 1991, has been building up an extensive network of Singapore-related people and organizations abroad. That network can provide a valuable entry to foreign business opportunities for Singaporeans and Singapore opportunities for foreigners. Though business promotion is not the sole aim of SIF, it would be a very effective ally in global networking.

Diaspora networks

There are 55 million overseas Chinese and more than a billion in China itself. One Chinese writer has described Chinese society as a tray of sand. "Each grain in the tray is not an individual but a family. They are held together ... by personal acquaintance, trust and obligation". Such ties have led to the creation of a Chinese diaspora which seeks to maximize benefits through its own networking across the oceans. For Singapore, with its long established relations with Chinese business communities in the region and beyond, it is a network of enormous value.

It is also possible to conceive of, though not on the same scale or depth, an Indian diaspora, and a Malay or Muslim diaspora. At this stage of Singapore's political and economic development, it seems both correct and profitable to tap into these ethnic connections for mutual benefit.

Flexible consortium

Lastly, I would like to explore an idea that has its origins in the Japanese networking model called *keiretsu*. Very briefly, *keiretsu* is a business grouping that is linked vertically or horizontally to achieve synergy and competitive advantage through collective strategy and tactics. The vertical *keiretsu* comprises suppliers and retailers under a large, industry-specific firm, while the horizontal *keiretsu* comprises companies from different industries, usually a bank, an insurance company, a trading company and a number of large manufacturing companies. Member firms are also linked by reciprocal stock ownership. The key advantages in this sort of business grouping are economies of scale, transfer of knowhow, quality control, reliability of service, long-term relationships and relative security of assets and markets.

In the Singapore context, what might be useful to develop is a "flexible" consortium that is vertically or horizontally integrated. One is suggesting a "flexible" approach because it is essential that each member of the consortium remains largely independent.

There are several reasons. First, Singaporean entrepreneurs still seem to prefer being their "own boss", with ultimate decision-making powers in their own hands. Thus, the cross ownership of consortium members should not negate the controlling power of the owner(s) and should be kept to nominal levels. Second, it is good for the health and competitiveness of the consortium for each member to be free to conduct business with others who are not consortium members and who could even be competitors of consortium members. Third, the consortium itself should remain flexible by not guaranteeing any member business that is not competitive. Fourth, and, perhaps, most importantly, this approach will avoid accusations of being protectionist against foreign competitors or of developing monopolies. One of the major criticisms against the *keiretsu* is that it is discriminatory to outsiders. The debate about whether Japanese practices are protectionist or not is still unsettled. But, whatever the case may be with the Japanese, Singapore simply cannot afford to get trapped in a protectionist debate.

In one sense the "flexible consortium" borrows some of the strengths of the fusion approach and the already well-established model of a joint venture, while avoiding some of their weaknesses. The joint venture is usually a one-off arrangement where partners come together in a formal and rigid ownership structure to carry out a single project. It does not, usually, exist beyond the project. The fusion business group, on the other hand, not only lacks the long-term commitment just like the joint venture, but also lacks the reciprocal ownership structure and its attendant obligations that the flexible consortium is designed to bring.

Thus, the "flexible consortium" offers one more avenue for exploration in deciding the future direction of corporate networking.

Success factors

Before closing, it might be useful to take a quick look at some fundamental success factors that seem to lie behind most corporate networking. There is mutual interest among network partners in what needs to be achieved and also a strong potential for mutual benefit in what is finally achieved. Partner firms or organizations also seem to have a natural affinity to each other. If the alliances are artificial or forced, they are unlikely to succeed. There is a shared belief in the long-term approach. It takes time to develop and nurture networks before they pay dividends. It is also over a period of time that network partners can balance out the ups and downs that are endemic to business ventures. And, finally, networking only works well when all partners stand to gain and not at the expense of one or more. It is not a win-lose but a win-win situation.

Trends, No. 30, *Business Times*, weekend edition, 27–28 February 1993

chapter 28

Creating a new urban élite for Singapore

Toh Thian Ser

Urban élites drive the growth of cities. They represent a cross-section of businessmen, professionals and others who are keen to see their city grow and to benefit from that growth. Singapore, as a rapidly growing city, has depended on the government and its civil servants to play the role of the urban élite. This has been done by cultivating top scholars and testing them in key positions to sieve out those who are bright but inefficient.

Singapore's ambitions are expressed, in their most publicized form, in *The Next Lap*. This book, while drawing a picture of the way our nation will grow, constantly returns to the constraints of geography. We are, after all, more a city-state than a nation, in terms of size, infrastructure, and the exposure to global and regional trends.

With apparent shortages in land and labour, we need to be far more international to continue our growth. Business is our lifeline but international business is usually one in which governments do not play an active role (other than regulation).

We are faced with a dilemma. Many of our best-run home grown companies are statutory boards and government-linked companies which have the potential for venturing abroad and taking Singapore's growth much further. Yet, their "government" labels can make it much more difficult for them to overcome obstructions put up by competitors based on accusations that they are owned by the Singapore Government and enjoy unfair advantage.

The government has indicated the need to nurture the growth of local entrepreneurs. However, Singapore has only a handful of home-grown, private-sector entrepreneurs with the ambition and funds for major international expansion. Most local firms are small and do not have the critical mass for rapid growth internationally. Also, many of our well-to-do prefer to own property assets rather than acquire stakes in long-term growth-oriented or leading-edge businesses.

How does Singapore speed up the pace of private enterprise, which is often the backbone of urban élites in other countries, when the pool of domestic entrepreneurs appears to be locked into government-linked companies and statutory boards?

We ought to examine the feasibility of transferring government ownership of those companies or statutory boards with profit/market orientation to their employees. Management-and-employee buy-outs will allow these companies to de-link from the government. Yet, they will still have Singapore's interests at heart if the decades of institutional development of these executives (in the 1970s and the 1980s) have been well executed.

In other words, their values and their loyalty will be to Singapore and they can be trusted to make more money for Singapore. This removal of government linkage, yet allowing well-trained former civil servants to own a significant portion of these companies, will allow Singapore companies to enter into a period of rapid international growth.

Management buy-outs should be allowed even for listed government-linked companies such as SIA, DBS, Keppel and Sembawang. The government still holds substantial stakes in these companies. Perhaps it is time to de-link officially the government, and the ownership and management of these companies and see if a close and informal alliance develops between our civil servants-turned owner-managers and the government. Such informal alliances are seen in Japan and South Korea although the nature of the linkage varies from country to country.

In some cases, the market capitalization of these companies is so large that it is beyond the ability of key managers to own substantial stakes. Instead, stock options have been offered to encourage ownership. Such schemes should be redesigned to make for more substantial ownership and much longer time-frames before the stock, purchased through the exercise of these options, can be sold. If these owner-managers are required to hold on to their shares for 10 to 20 years, they will be forced to adopt longer-term strategies for the internationalization of their companies. Perhaps they should be allowed to use their CPF savings when exercising these options.

If the principle of equity demands it, let all employees enjoy the opportunity to acquire stakes and provide long-term financing for those who need it. The priority, however, is for key managers to become substantial owners. This creates a new urban élite in Singapore, made up of businessmen who have imbibed the values that the Singapore Government has espoused over many years. They are given the opportunity to become very wealthy as they lead Singapore abroad. Within 15 to 25 years, this can give rise to new strong business families as seen in many other countries. Such families also tend to form the philanthropic core for a blossoming of the arts and concern for the welfare of less well-to-do Singaporeans, as was the case with entrepreneur-philanthropist Mr Lee Kong Chian.

If this succeeds, and a decade should be sufficient for the first indications to show, the government's role would be substantially altered. It will focus on regulation, ensuring that the new owner-managers of these companies comply with the requirement to grow quickly across borders and work closely with government planners on major areas of activity, both economic and social.

The separation of its role as a regulator from its role as an owner of assets will help the government to avoid the perception that it is a money-grabbing, wealth-accumulating agency. Conflicts of interest will also be reduced.

The government would be in an even stronger position to build Singapore as an international (perhaps global?) city. One of its key tasks would be to create the conditions for Singapore to thrive as a global/international city. These conditions include the following:

- First-class telecommunication and transport infrastructures. (We already have these).
- An environment for developing and nurturing international brands, i.e. products and services in international market segments which can be recognized as Singaporean (as Swatch is recognized as a Swiss product all over the world, or association of the Singapore Girl with our national airline).
- A lifestyle, both physical and cultural, which makes living in this city attractive and safe. (For the man-in-the-street, we are already one of the safest cities in the world).
- A redistribution of wealth and, more importantly, the creation of opportunities for workers in the lower-income groups and their children to move upwards.
- Job opportunities for skilled workers and professionals who enjoy cross-border appeal.

If these conditions can be met, Singapore will attract members of the urban élite of other cities. It may then become more important to focus on our cosmopolitan nature rather than on differences in ethnicity. This does not mean that ethnic traditions and values are ignored. Rather, that they are developed within the context of a cosmopolitan outlook. Paris, for example, is an international city with a cosmopolitan, yet distinctly French, flavour.

Policies such as the emphasis on bilingualism should not be discouraged but re-interpreted in the light of the objective of making Singapore a major, international city. Bilingualism should still be encouraged and people should learn more than one language, with the second not necessarily being the mother tongue. I believe we have enough Chinese Singaporeans who will keep Mandarin as our mother tongue as is the case with Malay for Malay Singaporeans and Tamil for Indian Singaporeans. However, we need to substantially broaden the study of French, German, Japanese — and also Malay as the regional language — among the future members of our urban élite.

If moderation and subtle adjustments to existing policies make Singapore more of a global city, it will lead to greater mobility of urban élites in and out of Singapore.

The ability to achieve a net increase in the urban élite would probably ensure a core rate of growth higher than the 4–5 per cent planned for Singapore over the long-term. This is because our city would become a draw for top-notch bankers, traders, marketers, designers, software developers, research scientists (with a commercial bent) and other creative businessmen. The high level of investment in tertiary education already evident in Singapore helps to establish a climate to attract such people.

Our recent emphasis on the development of the arts is a necessary condition for our growth as an international city. Although Western art is perceived to be desirable for teaching our young artists, we should allow for the development of the arts of ASEAN. Just as Hong Kong has gained recognition as a modern Chinese city, should Singapore aim to be the modern ASEAN city? It can distil the best of ASEAN traditions, ranging from Thai art forms to Filipino and Malay culture in the many ways in which they are now expressed. There are many great artists and artistes waiting to be discovered in ASEAN. Could Singapore become their impresario?

The various issues discussed above form a loosely laid mosaic which, if it challenges members of our current urban élite, could be put together to form a strategy to develop Singapore as an internationally-recognized global city.

Trends, No. 16, *Sunday Times*, 29 December 1991

chapter **29**

Privatization may not be the best answer

Anne Booth

Singapore's sustained economic success since the early 1960s has propelled it into the ranks of the high-income countries and, in terms of per capita gross domestic product (GDP), now places it just behind New Zealand and Australia. Yet the decline in national income experienced by Singapore in 1985 served as a warning that sustained economic growth could not be taken for granted. The 1986 report of the committee established by the government of Singapore to set out new directions for the economy found that the recession of the mid-1980s was due to both external and internal factors.

The report went on to recommend a number of reforms in economic policy-making in Singapore, emphasizing particularly the wage system, the tax regime, and policies to enhance the "overall business efficiency of firms". Most of the recommended reforms were implemented speedily and, by 1987, the rate of economic growth had recovered to almost 9 per cent per annum. How much of the continued growth in Singapore since 1987 has been due to domestic economic reforms and how much to the improved international environment is difficult to say, although both no doubt played a significant role.

The committee's report was, however, criticized by an academic economist for failing to tackle the problem of macroeconomic policy co-ordination. It was argued that a major reason for the erosion of competitiveness in the 1980s was that the main instruments of government policy were all combining to push up domestic costs; not only were wages and wage-related costs growing rapidly but the Singapore dollar was appreciating. It was concluded that there "needs to be a clear idea of instruments and objectives, and the effect of each instrument on the major economic variables".

The criticism that major government interventions in the Singapore economy were poorly co-ordinated, while certainly supported by evidence of the early 1980s, appears to contradict another frequent criticism that the government has been too dominant in Singapore and what is needed is not policy co-ordination but rather an across-the-board reduction in the economic role of government in the country. This line of argument appeared to receive considerable support in the 1986 report of the Economic Committee, which was established to determine the cause of the growth slow-down and chart new directions for the Singapore economy. It was argued that the very success of so many government-owned enterprises tended to stifle entrepreneurship, and what was needed was a programme of "long-term divestment" of public enterprises to the private sector. There was also a need to ease the regulatory environment in order to "encourage greater private sector initiative".

While the report was no doubt responding to an oft-repeated complaint that Singapore has not fostered the kind of free-wheeling entrepreneurs who flourish in more liberal Asian environments, such as Thailand and Hong Kong, it must be conceded that this is, by international standards, a very odd reason for advocating privatization. It is agreed universally that public enterprises in Singapore have been extremely well-managed and are, for the most part, very profitable. The kind of mismanagement all too familiar in many parts of the developing world (and not unknown in the OECD countries) has been virtually absent in Singapore.

Furthermore, the Singapore Government does not need the budget revenues which large-scale privatization would bring. Why then tamper with what are obviously well-managed and efficient public utilities, which make a considerable contribution to Singapore's very high aggregate rate of savings?

One experienced foreign observer of the Singapore scene has argued that the greatest need is not for the government to sell existing enterprises to the private sector, but to have less control of the economy. What is meant by government control? The ratio of government expenditure to GDP in Singapore is not particularly high by other Asian standards, and has fallen very steeply since 1987. The share of the government sector in fixed capital formation is also not very high in comparison with other parts of Asia. What is very high is the share of the public sector in total savings.

In part this may be due to the high prices charged by public monopolies which contribute to their high surpluses (profits), which is turn contribute to high savings. But if the charges are that public utilities are "too high", then the need is for more rather than less regulation of public utility pricing. There may be a case for selling off some of the many wholly or partially state-owned enterprises which are competing directly with private sector firms, but only if this leads to increased industrial efficiency. If such firms are well and profitably managed, they are probably enhancing rather than reducing the competitiveness of Singapore's economy.

It seems fair to conclude that the recent literature on the desirable role of government in the Singapore economy provides no compelling reason for large-scale divestment of public enterprises or for any marked "reduction" in the role of government in the economy. Indeed it could as well be argued that it is precisely the high performance standards set by the public sector in Singapore which have led to the country's impressive growth record over the past 25 years.

The rapid recovery of the economy since 1985 seems to support the proposition that it was not the "heavy hand" of government which led to the downturn of the mid-1980s, but rather the combination of unfavourable external circumstances and domestic policies which aggravated rather than mitigated their impact. This conclusion is an important one in that Singapore offers significant lessons to the other countries in ASEAN (and indeed to other parts of the developing world including the countries of eastern Europe). Governments in all these countries are faced with the problem of inefficient public enterprises.

Trends, No. 18, *Sunday Times*, 23 February 1992

chapter 30

Domestic enterprises: levelling the playing field

Tay Kheng Soon

Singapore's economic success over the past two decades has, in large measure, been due to the attraction and mobilization of multinational corporation (MNC) investments and their linkages to foreign markets. This has been paralleled by the state corporate sector and its progeny. However, this process seems to have marginalized local small and medium-sized enterprises (SMEs).

The time has probably come to do some rethinking, and to prune and level the domestic playing field. Some new creative ideas and appropriate structures are necessary to provide for small enterprises which clearly have a role to play in a modernizing Singapore.

Our typical SME is run on a shoe-string, a fact that makes it easy, from the corporate viewpoint, to be dismissive of such enterprises. The danger is that this attitude is self-validating: it leads to the creation of a permanent underclass. Yet, this need not and should not be so. It is often the small activities that provide the variety and the spice of life in any culture. The *char kway teow* sellers and the *karung-guni* men have and still do contribute much to the glue that defines the Singaporean. The *karung-guni* men should be given a national award rather than be looked down upon as an underclass.

The existence of the dismissive attitude and low regard of the SME sector, since it does not fit any of the criteria of the corporatist-administrator, was confirmed by Kenichi Ohmae's answer to my question, put to him at the National Business Forum 91, on his views of what to do with SMEs: "Kill them! I have no sympathy for them, but pay lip service."

Clearly, Ohmae reflects the corporatist view which is self-congratulating. Not only will this attitude affect SMEs negatively, but I also believe that it will ultimately erode the kind of social and cultural environment that is part of the glue that holds us as a nation together. If this kind of policy continues to be pursued it will systematically deplete what little intrinsic cultural glue there now exists in Singapore and replace it with artificial and cloying imitations of other people's excellence. Those authentic lifestyles and services which we all share in common are already being changed beyond recognition. The conscious and subconscious basis of our collective way of life is being lost unnecessarily in the name of progress. As the glue of everyday life is dissolved, it is being replaced by superficial foreign ideals — be they a brand of Imperial-China Chineseness, or Middle-Eastern Arabic styles, or Euro-American pop. The paradox is that in investing only in the big, we will lose our own intrinsic identity. The antidote is to invest also in our own small enterprises because in it is contained our essence.

In the realm of physical planning and design in realizing the utility of small enterprises, I have some suggestions to make and this line of thought is not restricted to just physical planning.

For now, let us first elaborate only on the opening up of opportunities for SMEs on marginal lands. Small developers have increasingly shown an interest in the possibility of allowing marginal lands to be developed with profit-generating uses in mind with small capital and plenty of entrepreneurial initiative. To do this, we need to have a dualistic policy in Singapore — one for the global corporate sector and the other for the local sector.

The two policies are not contradictory. The open free-market policy need not apply in the same way to the domestic sector which, by definition, is outside the international corporate sector and therefore does not affect our free-trade stance. As to objections of coddling local enterprises, let us just say that the fastidious Singaporean customer will ensure quality and cost effectiveness from our own SMEs.

A dualistic policy arises from different philosophical premises than those which apply to the MNC and corporate sectors. The philosophical premises of enhancing small enterprises begin from the view that they are already operating at an optimum level, low as it is. What they need are appropriate provisions designed to enhance their present operations. For example, why is it necessary to "upgrade" a *satay* stall? The stall is already operating at optimum and within a style that is its essence. And the character of the operation is part of its appeal; to transform it will result in its loss of identity and its cultural significance.

Furthermore, location represents capital for small operations. Given a good location, a business will thrive, and this will encourage the small entrepreneur to make improvements. It is important that essential features of Singapore's SME landscape carry over into the future and that change occurs within a continuum. What low-cost enterprises need is infrastructure support of a type that suits their operation.

The hawker centres of today, while fulfilling basic needs, are unattractive places and do not bring out the character-value of the stalls or celebrate the social habit of eating out. Hawker centres should be linear along well-trafficked routes and in parks. Our present rules and regulations and concepts make it impossible for small operations such as a *satay* stall to continue to operate except in large agglomerations. This, surely, is out of character for this type of operation and discontinuous with our way of life.

Rules and regulations

The rules and regulations governing developments when applied to small enterprises tend to work against small investors. This need not be so within a dualistic administrative philosophy where small investments in appropriate locations are regarded as valuable in providing for entrepreneurship and fulfilling a service which the population wants. For example, small wall-shops, coffee and tea kiosks as well as various kinds of allotments for marginal economic activities, if located in interstitial lands in the housing estates at strategic locations along footpaths and other well-trafficked locations, can provide livelihood and entrepreneurship potential for small business and, at the same time, continue a cultural practice.

If, however, such facilities are allocated through public tender, the resulting land-cost component will be higher, thereby taking away a part of the available capital for the operation. A better way to reward the initiative of small enterprises is to award good waste sites to those who have identified them and who wish to invest. These individuals within these enterprises know better than planners where the right sites are to be found. If there is more than one proposal for a site, then balloting would be a fair way to decide allocation. To avoid inflating the land cost and to be equitable, the land price can be fixed according to a formula based on a percentage of estimated business turnover. In this way, the landowner, being the government, is seen to be a partner in the operation rather than as a land profiteer. Here it is important that the land price generated in the corporate sector is not imported into the domestic sector.

For larger leftover sites with better economic potential, but still not attractive to large corporations to bother with, such as small odd-shaped lands left over from road-widening or from other infrastructural developments, the land price can be fixed as an average of recent transactions or based on the government's fixed land acquisition cost based on 1983 prices, whichever is the lower.

Often, traffic, pedestrian congestion or health reasons preclude the use of marginal lands for small developments. This can be overcome through licensing which can stipulate appropriate conditions. Overall aesthetic design of facilities in marginal lands can be a service provided by the Singapore Institute of Architects.

The cost and cultural benefits of implementing the foregoing suggestions for the lower sector of the working population are so great for so small an investment that not to implement them can only be explained in terms of oversight.

Trends, No. 17, *Sunday Times*, 26 January 1992

chapter 31

When will Singapore become a developed country?

Norbert Wagner

A rose is a rose, is a rose, is a rose ... But, is a developed country a developed country, a developed country ...? Apparently not quite, if the recently fashionable topic for speculation among Singaporeans and non-Singaporeans alike is any evidence. Is Singapore already a member of the group of developed countries? If not, when will it join the ranks of this élitist group?

Singapore, no doubt, has done very well economically over the past 25 years. In fact, over the past decade alone, gross national product (GNP) rose at an average rate of over 7 per cent per annum. And between 1987 and 1989 average GNP growth rates almost reached 10 per cent a year. Based on that particular quantifiable indicator Singapore is a truly developing country in the strictest sense.

Its performance certainly contrasts with many so-called developing countries elsewhere in Asia, in Africa, and in South and Central America which are in fact non-developing or even declining.

Yet, high growth rates in themselves do not say much about the level of development. Here per capita income or per capita GNP are more appropriate indicators. As a result of high GNP growth and low population growth, Singapore's per capita GNP increased substantially from US$3,830 in 1979 to about US$10,000 in 1989. This is the third highest GNP per capita in Asia, surpassed only by Japan and Hong Kong (disregarding Brunei, which is a special case).

Moreover, with a GNP per capita of US$12,000 Singapore fares far better than countries like Ireland, Spain, and Portugal, and follows closely behind Italy and Great Britain — countries categorized as developed. But does this make Singapore a developed country?

Answering the question involves the tricky problem of defining what development actually means and where to draw the borderline between developed and underdeveloped. (The latter term more accurately defines the actual status of Third World countries than the term "developing", which, as we saw above, is a mere euphemism.)

In their early days, the United Nations and the World Bank based their definition simply on per capita GNP. All countries below a certain level of GNP per capita were termed developing, while those above were termed developed or industralized countries. Very soon it was realized that such an approach was too crude to capture the vast differences among more than 100 countries.

As a result, a considerable number of categories have developed, but the basis for the categorization remains GNP per capita. For instance, countries are now grouped into least developed, low income, middle income (subdivided into lower and upper), newly industrializing, dynamic Asian, and so on.

But the prime reason for these subdivisions was not to reach a clearer understanding of the development level of a particular country, but rather to serve as a base for making individual countries eligible for specific aid and trade privileges. That is why, for instance, Myanmar in 1988 termed it a success to be downgraded into the list of the least developed countries.

The deficiencies of GNP per capita as an indicator of development are pretty obvious: measuring GNP is not that easy; nor is measuring the size of the population. International comparisons have to apply an exchange rate, but which one? Average GNP per capita says nothing about income distribution (in Brunei, for example).

Hence, various other development indicators have been created, such as the "Physical Quality of Life Indicator" conceived by a British researcher or the "Human Development Index" developed by the United Nations Development Programme. The latter, for instance, comprises life expectancy, literacy rate, and gross domestic product.

There is little argument that these variables are important elements of people's well being. But the country ranking according to that indicator is rather unsatisfactory: Vietnam ranks ahead of Indonesia and Morocco; Singapore behind South Korea, Poland, and Argentina; and the United States behind Ireland and Spain!

And what about the relevance of political, social, and cultural indicators? How do these affect the standard of living? How can they possibly be measured? Where does one draw the line between developed and underdeveloped as far as these aspects are concerned?

So, should one give up trying to seek an adequate definition of development and of the borderline separating developed from underdeveloped countries? Perhaps. After all, many multilateral organizations simply list countries without attaching a developmental status.

However, new concepts have emerged which have yet to be adequately recognized by the academic world and which may well lead to a breakthrough in development economics. One of these truly imaginative concepts suggests using the relation between the number of cars to the number of bicycles as an indicator of development.

By this measurement, there is little doubt that Singapore is a developed country, but what of the Netherlands and Denmark, where the older mode of transport is still very much in vogue? As an alternative, the quality of tapped water has been put forward. But then how should one conceptualize the French preference for bottled water?

The most imaginative and revolutionary indicator suggested so far is probably whether the drivers of public buses are younger or older than the buses they drive. The announcement by a Singapore bus company that it was planning to buy seven hundred new buses could well be seen as a serious effort to turn Singapore into a developed country very soon.

Surprisingly, given the otherwise omnipresent striving for excellence and for being No. 1 in every endeavour, Singaporean officials have been cautious or even reluctant to acknowledge that Singapore has already attained the status of a developed country.

Is it because being a developed country brings with it not only prestige but also burdens and responsibilities? Is it because developed countries don't receive aid from other countries, but, on the contrary, are expected to grant aid to poorer ones? Is it because developed countries don't receive trade preferences but instead have to compete with other developed countries on an equal footing?

Is it because they themselves face demands from developing countries to concede trade preferences? Is it therefore advantageous for Singapore to wait a little longer before declaring itself a developed country?

Trends, No. 1, *Straits Times*, 27 September 1990

Contributors

The editor

Derek da Cunha is a Senior Fellow at the Institute of Southeast Asian Studies, and Editor of *Trends*.

The contributors

Anne Booth is Professor of Economics (with reference to Asia) at the School of Oriental and African Studies, University of London.

David Chan Kum Wah is a Lecturer in the Department of Philosophy, National University of Singapore.

Chua Beng Huat is a Senior Lecturer in the Department of Sociology, National University of Singapore.

Janadas Devan is a literary critic who has studied and taught in the United States.

Philip Jeyaretnam is a lawyer and a novelist.

Geraldine Heng is an Assistant Professor in the Department of English at the University of Texas, Austin.

Russell Heng is a Fellow at the Institute of Southeast Asian Studies.

John Keung is Manager (Physical Planning) at the Urban Redevelopment Authority.

Stella Kon is a Singaporean playwright.

Sanjay Krishnan, formerly a Senior Tutor in the Department of English Language and Literature at the National University of Singapore, is a doctoral student at Columbia University, New York.

Lee Gek Ling is a Lecturer in the English Language Proficiency Unit at the National University of Singapore.

Liak Teng Kiat is a Fellow at the Institute of Southeast Asian Studies.

Liew Kim Siong is a public relations consultant with a private sector firm. His article was written whilst a Master's student in the Department of Sociology, at the National University of Singapore.

P. Lim Pui Huen is a Research Fellow at the Institute of Southeast Asian Studies, and an Associate Editor of *Trends*.

Ling Mei Lim is a free-lance writer concerned with cultural and educational issues.

Lily Zubaidah Rahim Ishak, formerly a Visiting Associate at the Institute of Southeast Asian Studies, is with Sydney University.

Arun Mahizhnan is a Senior Research Fellow at the Institute of Policy Studies.

G.L. Ooi is a Senior Research Fellow at the Institute of Policy Studies.

P.G. Raman is a Senior Lecturer at the School of Architecture, National University of Singapore.

Tay Kheng Soon, a local architect, is principal partner of the firm Akitek Tenggara II.

Toh Thian Ser is an Associate Professor and Vice-Dean in the School of Accountancy and Business, Nanyang Technological University.

Raj Vasil is Reader in Politics at Victoria University, Wellington, New Zealand.

Norbert Wagner heads the Konrad Adenauer Foundation's office in Moscow.

Walter Woon is an Associate Professor and Vice-Dean in the Faculty of Law at the National University of Singapore.

Yao Souchou is a Research Fellow at the Institute of Southeast Asian Studies.

Robert Yeo is Senior Lecturer in the School of Arts, Division of Language, Literature and Arts, National Institute of Education, Nanyang Technological University.